A HISTORY OF TRAMWAYS

A HISTORY OF TRAMWAYS

From Horse to Rapid Transit

R. J. BUCKLEY

DAVID & CHARLES

NEWTON ABBOT LONDON

NORTH POMFRET (VT) VANCOUVER

ISBN 0 7153 6641 6

Library of Congress Catalog Card Number 74-76196

Set in 11 on 13 pt. Bembo and Photoset and printed in Great
Britain by REDWOOD BURN LIMITED, Trowbridge & Esher
for David & Charles (Holdings) Limited, South Devon House,
Newton Abbot, Devon

Published in the United States of America by David & Charles
Inc., North Pomfret, Vermont 05053

Published in Canada by Douglas David & Charles Limited,
132 Philip Avenue, North Vancouver, B.C.

CONTENTS

The actual historical origin of tramways lies in the United States of America, a fact which was recognised for years afterwards by the name given to them in many European countries. In Frankfurt-am-Main, for example, when the introduction of tramways was being debated in the 1860s, they were referred to as *amerikanische eisenbahn*, and as late as 1885 the Brussels tramways were still being described as *Chemins de Fer Americains*, or American railways. Perhaps this is one of the first examples of a European invention that was developed and commercialised by the Americans and later re-exported by them. They, of course, do not use the word tramway at all, but refer to it as a street railway; and probably the legislators of New York State did not realise that they were authorising anything other than a railway when, on 25 April 1832, they passed an act permitting the New York and Harlaem Railroad to lay a line north of 23rd Street for passenger or goods transport 'by the power and force of steam, of animals, or of any mechanical or other power, or of any combination of them which the said Company may choose to employ'. They soon seem to have realised, however, that a railway in the street was something which needed second thoughts, and later regulations forbade the use of anything other than horse power, although the company actually did use steam engines for a while in defiance of this edict. Construction of the line must have proceeded very rapidly, for the first horse cars were running by 14 November 1832, and the official opening took place on 26 November 1832, when *John Mason*, named after the president of the company, ran from Prince Street to 14th Street in New York City. The car resembled an early railway carriage; it had side doors above double running boards, and three carpeted compartments each with ten quilted seats. There may also have been up to thirty places on a central roof seat. The vehicle was made by John Stephenson, a New York coachbuilder, who later built up one of the largest tramcar construction businesses in the world.

There was no immediate rush to imitate this first example, apart from an isolated 4 mile suburban line, the New Orleans and Carrolton, which was opened in 1835; still operating, this is by far the oldest tramway in the world. The first moves towards establishing a tramway system, as opposed to an isolated line, took place in New York, where in 1851 the Sixth and Eight Avenue Railroad Companies both obtained franchises.

* *Transport History* 5 No 2 (1972)

This was the signal for the promotion of numerous other lines in the city, where the number of companies continued to increase until the 1890s, when a period of consolidation began. Outside New York, the first horse street railroad in Massachusetts opened at Cambridge in 1852 between Harvard College and Union Square, Somerville; this was a one-man business, in which the owner drove the only vehicle, an abandoned railway passenger car obtained from the Fichtburg Railroad. Other lines soon appeared in larger places, like Philadelphia in 1855, Boston in 1856, and Cincinnatti, Chicago and Pittsburgh in 1859. After that expansion proceeded apace, with horse railways springing up all over the United States. By 1875 in New York State alone there were eighty-seven street railway companies with 433 miles of track open, and the twelve of them within New York City were carrying almost 167 million people annually. This was double the total of ten years before, and even then the *New York Herald* had been complaining that the streetcars were too crowded: 'People are packed into them like sardines in a box, with perspiration for oil. The seats being more than filled, the passengers are placed in rows, down the middle, where they hang on by the straps, like smoked hams in a corner grocery'.

These were the problems of success, however, and by the end of the 1850s other countries were being persuaded of the benefits of street railways. There had actually been an exhibition line constructed in Vienna in 1840, and another in Brussels in 1854, but neither had any long term influence. The first permanent street tramway in Europe had a direct connection with the New York and Harlaem, for the promoter, M Alphonse Loubat, had worked with the latter company. In 1853 he laid an exhibition line in Paris, and regular service began in 1855. The line was laid to the non-standard gauge of 1.54m (5ft ½in), and was operated by very large and heavy vehicles. Loubat himself sold out to the Compagnie Generale des Omnibus in 1856, and apart from a separate line opened in the following year between Sèvres and Versailles, there was a considerable gap between the pioneer venture and any large scale development, just as there had been in America a quarter of a century before.

The next event in the story took place in England where a native inventor, William Joseph Curtis, obtained permission from the Liverpool Docks Company to run a service of 'railway omnibuses' along their dockside goods lines. The service ran for only nine months in 1859, then being withdrawn partly because the toll had been raised and partly because the docks company's own goods traffic was being disrupted by the other operators it had allowed on the line. The first English tramway to have a continuous existence until displaced by motor buses was nevertheless laid on the banks of the Mersey, between Woodside Ferry and Birkenhead Park. The Town Commissioners of Birkenhead gave George Francis Train, an American, permission to lay the track which was opened to traffic on 30 August 1860 with great ceremony. Train also laid lines in Darlington, the Potteries, just outside Liverpool in West Derby, and in London, where his three demonstration lines along Bayswater, Kennington and Victoria Roads were the first tramways in the capital. All of these had to be removed after a few months or years, apart from the Birkenhead line and that of the Staffordshire Potteries Street Railway Company between Hanley and Burslem, and even these had to be completely relaid in 1864. The reason was because Train insisted on using a type of track known as step rail which projected above the road surface so causing an obstruction. This was unfortunate, as his trams were the best road passenger vehicles which had been used in England up to this time, as the *Evening Standard* report on the opening of the Bayswater Road line on 23 March 1861 indicates: 'There were three carriages on the line, all beautifully fitted up and appointed. They were built by Messrs Prentice of Birkenhead, are exceedingly light and airy, and constructed to hold 24 passengers inside and 12 on the front and back'.

Train did make attempts to open lines in other places, such as Birmingham and Glasgow, but without success, and he soon left the country, a disappointed man. As in other countries there was a period of years in which little progress was made. A rather curious line was opened in Salford, in Lancashire, in 1861, where John Greenwood operated vehicles on 'Haworth's patent perambulating system'. This involved ordinary buses running on two smooth outer rails guided by a 'perambulator' wheel running in a central grooved rail, it being possible to raise or lower this wheel by a rod passing through the footboard, so the vehicle could run as a tram or as a bus as required. The next street tramway in Europe was opened by an English company in Copenhagen in 1863, using eight double-deck cars supplied by one of the most famous early tramcar builders, Starbuck of Birkenhead. At about this time the first tram lines were opened in a number of countries, including such cities as Montreal, Toronto and Sydney in 1861, and Berlin and Vienna in 1865. Widespread adoption of horse tramways did not, however, take place until the 1870s, an expansion which in the United Kingdom was signalled by the passing of the 1870 Tramways Act, which provided a general legal framework for establishing new lines. Before that it had been necessary either to get the permission of the local authority, as with Train's lines, or to obtain a special Act of Parliament, which had been done in one or two cases, including the Landport and Southsea Tramway which was opened in 1865 to carry boat passengers between Portsmouth Town Station and Clarence Pier, and the much more important Liverpool tramways which opened in 1869. This was the first line to be authorised by Parliament for local transport, and the service was inaugurated between Exchange and Dingle and on the inner circle on 1 November 1869, using sixteen trams built in New York by John Stephenson's firm.

The Tramways Act was the signal for a wave of promotions and construction. First off the mark was the Plymouth, Stonehouse and Devonport Tramways Co Ltd, but other companies were soon formed, including one in Dublin, which opened the first street tramway in Ireland in 1871 (there had been a horse-worked railway branch at Fintona since 1854). London's first permanent lines, actually opened under powers granted in 1868, appeared at about the same time. The very first was opened on 2 May 1870 by the Metropolitan Street Tramways Co between Brixton and Kennington Church, followed only a week later by the North Metropolitan route from Whitechapel to Bow. The third pioneer company, the Pimlico, Peckham and Greenwich, opened a line between New Cross and Blackheath Hill in December, but amalgamated with the Metropolitan Street that same month to form the London Tramways Co. By 1873 there were 42 miles of route in London. Several other cities opened tramways in the early 1870s, so that by 1876 there were nearly 220 miles of tram route in the United Kingdom. This was still very little as compared with the United States, of course, but the pace quickened in the later seventies and in the eighties so that by the end of the decade all major cities and many small towns had their tramways. The pattern on the European continent, and throughout the world, was much the same—a slow start, followed by an increasingly wide penetration of horse tramways. From 1880 to 1895 they virtually monopolised city transport, and in many towns they continued to do so until after the turn of the century.

Although the basic principles of the horse tramway might appear very simple, in fact a considerable amount of thought went into both the track and the cars. To deal with the track first, this had not only to be capable of supporting and guiding the trams, but also of giving a smooth passage to other traffic. The first street tramways in New York used rails with a very wide and deep groove, and with a ridge projecting above the road surface, which were, of course, very inconvenient to road vehicles, whilst the grooves tended to get blocked by pebbles and mud. To counteract these disadvantages a new type of rail was introduced into Philadelphia in 1855. The principle of this step rail, the type used later by G. F. Train, was that ordinary vehicles could run along a plate laid level with the road surface, whilst the trams ran on a raised edge on the outside of the plate. The Philadelphia rail consisted of 5in plates laid at a gauge of 5ft 2in with a $\frac{7}{8}$in step, and some later rail used in New York was as wide

Below   A single-deck horse car in York Road, Leeds, posed with its proud crew shortly after the opening of the line in 1871. Note the old-style arched roof [*Leeds City Transport*

as 8in. In Toronto similar rail was used on the English wagon gauge of 4ft 10⅞in to avoid the difficulty and expense of having vehicles travel on the right of way with one wheel on the track and the other wearing a rut in the cedar paving. However, although the step rail had a vogue in America, where bad road surfaces led to other road traffic using the tracks where it could, the track was unpopular in other countries because of the inconvenience caused to cabs and wagons attempting to cross the track, which projected above the road surface, and because the plate did not give a very good foothold for horses.

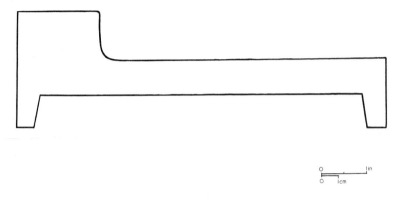

This example of step rail was used in New York from 1860; it had a total width of 8in and a step 1in above street level

Another form of experimental track was the crescent rail, basically formed from a bar of iron with the two upper edges cut off, the bar being screwed to longitudinal timbers and laid flush with the street. The space left at the edges provided a very narrow groove for the flanges of the tram's wheels, but experience proved that this space was not adequate, as it could easily be blocked. Crescent rail was used in the United States, on some suburban lines in Belgium, and experimentally in Liverpool in 1865, although it was not adopted for the permanent lines there. The most obvious type of track to use for tramways was Vignoles rail, the type used on railways, and this was in fact employed on the newly opened tramways in Moscow in 1874. (There was also a tramway rail patented by H. Vignoles in 1879 and used in Tottenham and Stoke-on-Trent in 1881; this was not railway track, but grooved girder rail supported in chairs). By the following year 60 miles were open on this system, which involved a rail projecting slightly above the road surface with a groove cut in the paving on the inner edge. Counter rails were used only at points and crossings. The great advantage was that less than half the tractive effort needed to haul a tram along grooved rail was needed, but in busier cities the obstruction to other traffic was too great. Another method of using railway track was adopted in Lille and Geneva, where a rail and counter rail were laid in exactly the same way as at a railway level crossing. This was probably quite effective from the point of view of both the trams and the road traffic, but it must have been expensive to lay two rails where one would do, and the system did not catch on.

One of the more eccentric solutions to the track problem was patented by a Mr Edge in the later 1870s. The rails were hollow and had holes drilled in them along the top. Special wheels fitted to the tramcar had studs at similar intervals, and these engaged the holes, so keeping the car on the track. Cars needed studded wheels along one side only. A quarter mile experimental track was laid in a figure of eight formation at Birmingham, where it performed satisfactorily, and two $1\frac{1}{2}$-mile lines were actually put into service in Brunswick in 1879 and 1880. It was a typical example of an over-complex solution to a simple problem, something which happened frequently in the pioneer era of tramways.

The simple solution was the shallow grooved rail, which provided a surface flush with the road and an effective means of guiding the tramcar. Such a rail had been introduced as early as 1856 by C. L. Light, an Englishman who was involved with the first tramways in Boston, Mass. As we have seen, many American systems adopted the rival step rail, but in the United Kingdom and Europe the grooved rail soon became standard, as it did later in the Americas. The common form of the rail provided a shallow groove along one side of the rail to take the flange with the bearing surface outside. A variant of this was the centre groove rail, an American invention, which was used in Liverpool from 1877 when the original tracks became due for relaying. Its advantage was that the whole area of the rail not used for the groove could be used as a rolling surface, which made for steadier running, especially over points and crossings where some part of the rail was always in contact with the wheel. Special wheels with centre flanges were needed, and these were fitted to the cars as the ordinary wheels wore out. The first line to be relaid was the inner circle, and until all the lines were rebuilt the centre flange wheels were able to run on both side and centre grooved rail.

The running surface, therefore, came to be standardised as the shallow grooved rail. The second problem associated with the track was its means of support. First, wooden sleepers were employed, as on the railways, though the method of construction was rather different. Early tram rail, whether step or grooved, was usually made out of a fairly thin strip of iron which was not strong enough to support itself, as railway track was. Hence it was bolted, screwed or nailed to longitudinal sleepers, which were in turn attached to the usual transverse sleepers. These were laid to a depth of about one foot, packed with concrete, and the whole paved with wood or stone blocks. It soon became evident that this type of construction was not strong enough, and various patented designs of iron rails were produced. These included Joseph Kincaid's system, used in Sheffield and Bristol, Dawson's system of iron rails on cast iron sleepers used in Madras, and James Livesey's steel rails on stools bolted to cast iron plates which were used to replace the old wood supported lines in Buenos Aires. Eventually a standard form of steel girder rail was produced, like Vignole rail, but with a groove rolled into its head. So far as the United Kingdom was concerned, these had been patented as early as 1860, but had not been made then due to technical difficulties in rolling them. Later on another patent was taken out, by Messrs Winby and Levick, and the rail was used for the first time in Nottingham in 1878. After that the grooved girder rail soon became the norm, as it is today.

The most important advantage of tramways as compared with road vehicles was their lower rolling resistance, and much of the effort of tramway engineers was directed towards keeping this at a minimum. Unfortunately the most effective form of rail from other points of view, the shallow-grooved girder, involved considerably more resistance than railway track, both because it tended to fill with dirt and because the curves were much tighter. One method of easing cars round curves used by the Compagnie des Voies Ferrees Belges, one of the four companies operating in Brussels, involving a flat outer rail on curves and a slightly depressed running surface on the inner grooved rail. In Paris the Compagnie Generale used a particular type of car to deal with the same prob-

lem. The wheels on their large single-ended double-deckers were
flanged on one side only, and in addition the front wheels were pivotted
on a frame to which the horses were attached, which made it easier to
negotiate curves and also reduced the resistance to traction as compared
with ordinary cars. Another invention designed to help cars move freely

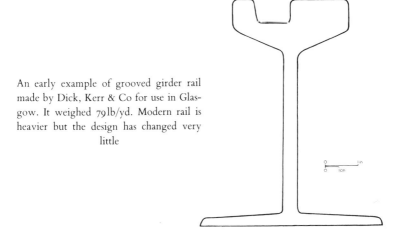

An early example of grooved girder rail
made by Dick, Kerr & Co for use in Glasgow. It weighed 79 lb/yd. Modern rail is
heavier but the design has changed very
little

round curves was the radial truck produced by James Cleminson, a
system occasionally found on the railway carriages of the period. This
involved three axles, the two outer ones having central pivots on which
they swivelled freely, whilst the central axle was on a frame which slid to
and fro, this being connected to the two outer wheels by 'articulated
radiating gear'. The result was that the two outer axles were deflected to
take up radial positions to suit the curve, and then restored to parallelism
on the straight, which reduced resistance and lessened the flange wear associated with the rigid wheelbase. According to D. K. Clark, from
whom these details are derived, such a car was used on the Dublin and
other tramways, but the system never seems to have been used at all
widely in the horse tram era.

Whilst many inventors were devoting their time and energy towards
keeping tramcars running easily on the rails, others were as busily en-
deavouring to take them off again! Early tramway promoters seem to
have been much struck by the idea of combining the advantages of trams

and omnibuses, and of being able to run the same vehicle both on and off the rails. Sometimes this was no doubt for reasons of economy, in others because the local authority would not allow the tracks to be laid to the end of the route. This was the case with Loubat's original line in Paris, for example, where the tramway was not allowed to go east of the Place de la Concorde. In 1866 the line was extended to the Louvre by changing the wheels at Cours de la Reine, and running as a bus route from there. William Curtis seems to have adopted a similar method on his Liverpool Docks service, where his vehicles were described as having 'moveable flanges', and of course there was also the nearby line at Salford. Such schemes seem to have been fairly common at one time, for in 1872 a new company, the Frederiksberg Sporvejsselskab, opened a route in Copenhagen from Smallegade to Kongens Nytorv, operated by what they called a 'Kiefler Omnibus', fitted in this case with a pony truck which could be retracted to enable it to run as a bus between Raadhusplads and Kongens Nytorv. And in Brussels the last company to be formed began operating in 1889 with *deraillables* trams. Both companies later turned over to orthodox trams, because as time went on it became clear that a tram needed to be designed differently from a bus if it was to realise its full potential.

Stephenson's first car looked rather like a contemporary railway carriage, but other early American streetcars were little different from the omnibuses of the time. They were single-ended, with the driver sitting high up at one end and passengers boarding from a step at the rear. This design led to difficulties in turning the vehicle at the end of its run, whilst it was inconvenient having the driver perched up on high, particularly if he was expected to collect the fares as well. So it was not long before vehicles which we would still recognise as tramcars were introduced. Built entirely of wood, strengthened here and there with metal ties, the cars ran on cast iron wheels, often mounted on large blocks of india rubber which were used as springs. The brakes, one of the tramcar's innovations, consisted of metal blocks applied by turning a wheel or handle mounted on each platform. The body was solidly constructed with benches down each side of the saloon. The sash windows could be raised, and above them was a row of curved or trefoil windows, often with ornamental glass in them. The roof was curved, with a sort of 'eyebrow' effect at the ends which provided space for a ventilator, sometimes supplemented by a row of five or six small windows along the side of the roof. It was this type of car which G. F. Train, following American practice, had built for his English lines between 1860 and 1862, except that two of them were double-deckers. The Birkenhead car builder, Geo Starbuck & Co, took up this design and continued to build it for some years.

The main problems with this type of car were inadequate light and ventilation and, above all, excessive weight. Improvements in these directions began to be made by American builders from about 1870, and in 1873 a major advance was made with the introduction of the monitor, or, as it is known in Europe, the clerestory roof, which provided a line of ventilators along the full length of the roof on both sides of a raised central section, making it much stronger than the older types. Larger saloon windows were also provided around this period with the sashes designed to drop into the sides. The newest American 22-seaters weighed only 38cwt, as opposed to the 50cwt of the older cars, and some even lighter cars built by Starbuck in the mid-1870s included a Sheffield 16-seater weighing 29cwt and a Naples 20-seater open car at only 21cwt. Open cars were extremely popular in North America for summer use, to a lesser extent in Western Europe, and hardly at all in the United Kingdom. The most common form of horse car throughout the world was the single-decker, either enclosed or open. The most obvious and widespread variation from this pattern was the double-decker. These were not common in the United States, although their car builders did construct some—Stephenson's, for example, supplied four to the first tramway in Adelaide, and also built a great many cars for the London companies. Britain, and places which were influenced by British practice, were the major market for double-deckers. Like the single-deckers, these were usually double-ended, the difference being that stairs gave access from each platform to the roof, where on the earliest cars two seats were placed back-to-back along the top deck. Bristol's first cars, for example, were equipped with these knifeboard seats, together with six window saloons, open-rung spiral staircases, and seating for 16 on each deck. Later cars in the fleet were larger, with seven windows, and with more substantial side protection on the upper deck as well as the new type of reversible transverse seating, known as garden seats, which later became standard for most double-deckers, although longitudinal benches were retained in the saloon.

A few undertakings, like the Adelaide and Suburban, operated single-ended double-deckers. The problem with these cars was how to turn them at the end of the journey. The Adelaide company used to install turntables at all its depots, these often being used not only for reversing, but also instead of points into the depot. On its second line, that to North Adelaide opened in December 1878, a balloon loop was installed at the Caledonian Hotel, the city terminus, but this was later replaced by a turntable, as the tight 'one-way' curve tended to wear the left-hand flanges too rapidly. Another horse tramway loop, incidentally, was to be found in a wide road at Camberwell Green on the London Southern Tramways.

Double-deck horse cars were rarely top covered, presumably because of the extra weight involved. Bristol had a few, but these were for use behind an experimental steam locomotive. Where covers were used they were not solid structures, but only awnings. Ten of the eleven Adelaide companies fitted these, together with curtains at the sides and end for use in bad weather. The exception was the Hindmarsh company, sheds of which were too low, and which had once had a car capsize in a gale.

Large fleets of double-deckers were unusual on the continent of Europe. Copenhagen's various companies all used them, with the exception of the Solvgadens Sporvejsselskab, probably following the example of the pioneer English line of 1863. Many other cities ran double-deckers to start with, but few kept them for long. Known as Imperials, such cars were operated in places like Munich, Frankfurt-am-Main and Vienna. Access to the knifeboard seat on the top deck of the Frankfurt cars was by steps projecting from the bulkhead with support from a vertical hand-rail, a process which, together with the problems associated with bad weather, caused the early purchase of American style single-deckers from a builder in Brussels. In Vienna light one-horse cars succeeded the original double-deckers of 1865, but by 1879 two-horse cars were again needed, and severe overcrowding forced the reintroduction of double-deckers by the Wiener Tramway Gesellschaft between 1894 and 1897.

American cars tended to be heavier than those used in Europe, but from the 1870s a new form of a light, one-horse car began to be introduced. Known as the bobtail this had only one platform, passengers boarding omnibus fashion from a step at the rear. Used in conjunction with a fare box, they could be operated by one man. Such economies meant that a more frequent service could be maintained, so being beneficial both to the company and to the passengers. Bobtails first appeared in New Orleans and began spreading in the northern United States in the 1870s. However, just as in Vienna, traffic later became too heavy for these small cars, and severe overcrowding made the bobtails extremely unpopular. By the 1880s most American lines were once again using the two-man, two-horse car.

Being single-ended such cars required a turntable or a loop at each terminus. With double-ended cars it was only necessary to uncouple the horses, walk round the car, and hitch them up again. However even this wasted time on a busy line, and various cars were designed which could be turned without the need for unhitching. One such was the balloon car designed by Henry Casebolt in 1871 for his City Front, Mission and Ocean Railroad in San Francisco. Characterised by its oval outline, the whole body could be swivelled on the stationary truck. The Eades Reversible Car, patented in 1877 and used in Salford, worked on a similar principle. This car, seating 16–18 passengers, was of a very light construction, the result of a light frame, wooden wheels and smaller axles than normal. This meant that only eight horses, instead of the usual eleven or twelve, were needed to keep it in operation—a considerable economy.

A great many special designs of horse car were produced for particular types of traffic. Tramways were often built in connection with amusement facilities, especially in the United States. In San Francisco the City RR Co ran to Woodward's Amusement Park, the owner of the latter being a promoter of the street railway company. For this service Woodward had a special 'Street Palace' car built by the Kimball Manufacturing Company. The *San Francisco News Letter* of June 1870 described the car in glowing terms—it 'is elegant in design, luxuriously fitted up with velvet carpets, and sofas extending the length of the car, upholstered in embroidered tapestry'. The car was decorated with frescoes, was ladies only, no smoking, no standing—and double the fare! Other types of special car included the sleeping cars built for the 90 mile route of the Tramway Rural near Buenos Aires, Argentina, and the first, second and third class funeral trams used in the same city. Some lines also had freight cars, including chicken, sheep, meat and gravel wagons.

Although the design of the horse tramcar itself was taken over almost unchanged into the early electric era, certain other aspects of the horse tramway were peculiar to itself. The most prominent feature of the depot would not be the car sheds, as on a tramway today, but the stables. This was because far more horses were needed than cars—the accepted ratio was 11:1. Some of the other ancillary buildings appear in this inventory of London's Chiswick depot when it was in the hands of the receiver in 1894—stabling for 140–170 horses, a three storey granary, fodder stores, sheds for 20 cars, 7 cottages arranged as 14 dwellings for workmen, a yard and an excercise ground. Special staff were also needed. For instance, the Adelaide and Suburban employed not only the obvious drivers and conductors, but also stablemen, responsible for 14 horses each, night watchmen, who also had to clean and grease the cars, blacksmiths, farriers, harness makers, car builders, painters, a colt breaker and a vet. For the employees hours were long and pay was low. On the Aberdeen system, for example, the men worked an average of $14\frac{1}{2}$hrs a day, with an hour off for breakfast and for dinner, tea being taken on the tram. It is true that they had three evenings off from 5.00 p.m. and there were no Sunday services. A driver's pay was 22s a week in his first year and 24s thereafter.

Another feature of horse tramways was the practice of indicating the route by colours. In many cases this was simply taken care of by the differing liveries of competing lines—in San Francisco, for example, the Omnibus RR ran yellow cars, the Central red, and Casebolt's line had a green livery. Where a larger company with several branches was involved one of two expedients was followed. Either the cars on each route were painted in an entirely different livery—again in San Francisco the North Beach and Mission RR ran yellow, red and blue cars on its three branches—or coloured symbols, together with coloured lights at night, might be used. This was the case on the ten routes of the Adelaide and Suburban, where, for instance, the Prospect route carried a red square during the day and green, red and white lights at night.

Most horse tramway undertakings were small-scale affairs, resulting in a large number of separate and competing lines in the larger cities. In 1873 eight companies operated in San Francisco with a total of only 42 miles of route between them, and cities like Berlin, Paris and London also suffered from an excessive number of competing lines. In the latter there were well over twenty undertakings, if one includes companies later taken over by others and the municipal corporations which operated horse tramways in the interim before electrification. In Brussels there were six companies, one operating steam trams, in the 1890s, and a like number in Copenhagen, whilst Adelaide, only a fairly small city, had no less than eleven. Smaller places, of course, like Cambridge, Exeter and Ipswich, usually only had one undertaking, although this was also true of some of the larger places, especially in Britain where there was strong pressure towards municipal control, and unified systems were to be found in such places as Bristol, Glasgow and Sheffield. There was also a number of towns with large systems in other countries, of course, especially as the need for mechanisation enforced consolidation, as it did, for example, in New York.

The place of foreign capital and expertise was quite important in the development of horse tramways. The pervasive American influence has already been noted, as has the fact that one of the first European tramways, in Copenhagen, was built by an English company. There are many other examples, including Frankfurt, where the tramways were founded by a Belgian group, as they were in Munich, where the manager was actually French. When the original company was replaced by the Munchner Trambahn AG in 1882 the new director was an Italian count!

So far as the financial success of horse tramways was concerned, as a general rule the larger companies did better than the smaller. In London the three main companies, the North Metropolitan, the London Street and the London Tramways did fairly well as they had gained powers for the most profitable districts, whilst the smaller companies which filled in the gaps were not always so successful. One of these, the West Metropolitan, went bankrupt in 1894 after falling into such a state of decay that pieces of broken track could be picked up in the street, whilst its cars were described as a 'museum of antiquities'. The London United, however, which took over the same lines managed to make a great success of them, eventually paying an eight per cent dividend.

However the horse tramway business was not one in which anyone was likely to make their fortune, and the high costs of operation, which limited profits, were one of the factors which impelled tramway operators to seek for an effective form of mechanical power. Normally eleven horses were required for each car in service—five pairs to work in shifts, and one spare in the stables. So an enormous number of horses was needed to service a relatively small fleet of cars—the North Metropolitan, for example, had 673 cars and 7167 horses in 1898. Tramway horses cost between £20 and £50, and had a working life of about four years, six months less than that of a bus horse. Some companies attempted to make do with less horses, like the Dewsbury, Batley and Birstall which had eight horses per car, but this probably actually increased costs as the horses were worn out sooner. Some of this company's horses had to be retired after only a year, and as a result its horsing costs were pushed up to 69 per cent of total expenditure, as compared to the average of 55 per cent. Mechanical traction showed promise of reducing these operating costs considerably, as well as of increasing revenue through higher speeds and greater capacity.

The other main reason for mechanisation was that horses were inherently unsuited to tramway work, as D. K. Clark recognised as early as 1878. For one thing they were subject to disease, and the close-packed stalls and communal feeding arrangements meant that this could easily escalate into an epidemic. One of the worst was the Great Epizootic which swept the eastern seaboard of North America in the winter of 1873, killing off thousands of horses and bringing operations to a halt in many cities. But even when healthy, horses were simply unable to do all that was demanded of them. The team was frequently unequal to the load, especially in hilly cities like San Francisco, and sometimes serious accidents could occur. In Edinburgh four horses were needed on the steepest sections, and even then those used on the worst line along Leith Walk had to be shifted to an easier route every few months to regain their strength, whilst two authorised lines were not attempted at all until cable traction became available. In a similar instance, tramway development in Aachen came to halt in 1889 as the gradients were too steep for horses. Distance was also a barrier, for people would not spend more than about 1½hr travelling to work, which meant a limit of nine miles at the horse's 6mph.

So for reasons of cost and efficiency it was only a matter of time before horses were replaced by some form of mechanical traction. The search for an effective means of locomotion took a long time, but by the 1890s the writing was on the wall. In the decade from 1888 to 1899 the percentage of horse track to total mileage in the United States fell from 91.4 to 4.2, and although the changeover tended to come slightly later in Europe and the United Kingdom, it was largely complete by 1914.

CHAPTER TWO

MECHANICAL TRACTION

FACED with the necessity of finding a mechanical substitute for horse traction, tramway engineers really only had one source of power to turn to, namely steam. The most obvious course of action was to imitate the by then highly successful railways and employ steam locomotives on tramways. Light locomotives had in fact been used on street tramways almost from the beginning, for the New York and Harlaem, despite the prohibition against mechanical power in its concessions, had four 20hp engines built in 1837–8. A later American inventor, Brennand, installed a small auxiliary motor on a horse tramcar in 1858 not to replace, but to assist the horses. It was in the following year, 1859, that the first steam-powered vehicle propelled solely by steam and designed expressly for tramway work was put into service.

This car, built by Messrs Grice and Long of Trenton, New Jersey, was self-contained in that both the motor and the passenger compartment were on the same chassis. The car had a bogie at the rear whilst the motor drove through a single axle at the front. Several were constructed and worked successfully on the Frankford and Southwark Passenger Railway in Philadelphia up to 1893. At peak hours the cars drew double-deck trailers, a combination which was probably unique, for though such trailers were common in Great Britain they were drawn by independent locomotives without passenger accommodation.

Most early steam tramcars were designed on this self-contained principle. At first motors were simply fitted to existing horse cars, or at least to cars built on the same principles. An early American car built by the Baldwin Locomotive Works of Philadelphia had a motor on an iron plate which was bolted to the wooden frame of the car. It was soon discovered that this type of construction was too weak, and the motor was fitted to an iron frame to which, with economy still in mind, existing car bodies could be attached. A much later Baldwin car of the 1890s was powered by a four-wheeled truck with a trailing bogie, and had three separate compartments for engine, baggage and passengers.

Another pioneer American car was built by A. B. Latta for the Cincinnatti tramways around 1860, whilst a small fleet of six cars built by Gilbert, Bush & Co and powered by Ransom engines were running in Philadelphia in 1876–7. The line used had many inclines and curves, and the cars did not cope well with these, slipping on a greasy mud of the city streets. In fact the combination type of car was never very successful, and the majority of steam tramways used locomotives hauling separate trailers.

However despite this the first steam tram to operate in England was a combined engine and carriage. Built by John Grantham, the car was an ordinary two-axled double-decker with an underfloor motor powered by two boilers placed in the centre of the saloon. The engine was tested in London in 1873, but was found to be underpowered and was reconstructed several times, eventually ending up on the Wantage tramway, where it opened the first permanent steam tramway service in the United Kingdom on 1 August 1876.

Experiments continued to be made for some years with self-contained cars. For example the Stirling and Bridge of Allan Tramways, a horse line opened in 1874, experimented with a car patented by Messrs Robertson and Henderson of Glasgow. Two private trials were made at night and a public run on Thursday 14 July 1878 when the return journey of 3 miles was made in a quarter of an hour. The car, according to contemporary accounts, was like an ordinary car inside and out with no greater vibration or inconvenience than normal. The boiler was at one end, and the engine and steam tank under the floor between the axles. The water capacity was 200gal, sufficient for 12–14 miles. The car could be driven from either end, whilst powerful brakes could stop it at its highest speed in less than its own length. On level lines the engine was wrought as a compound one, enabling steam to be economised; but while ascending steep inclines, by the motion of a handle, all three cylinders could be supplied with steam direct from the boiler. However this car never came to anything, and the experiment ended ignominiously, as so many did, when the secretary of the tramway company was served with a Court of Session interdict, on the instance of Lord Abercromby, to desist from running steam cars.

The only really successful use of self-contained steam tramcars was in Paris, where single-deck cars to the design of W. R. Rowan were used from 1889 to 1910. Rowan's cars were also used in small numbers in other countries, including Denmark, where 12 cars hauled a similar number of open-sided trailers on a line from Copenhagen to the seaside resort of Klampenborg. However the motor cars were not very satisfactory and were later rebuilt into double-deck trailers to be towed by more orthodox steam locomotives. In Paris also the Rowan type cars were later replaced by Serpollet and Purrey steam cars, which were massive four-wheel double-deckers, some of which survived until 1914.

The alternative to the combination car was a locomotive and trailer as on the steam railways. Having an independent locomotive meant that much larger and more efficient engines could be designed, whilst at the same time removing them from the immediate vicinity of the passengers. Such locomotives were usually known as dummies because they were made to look as much like ordinary tramcars as possible in order to avoid frightening the horses which still provided the motive power for most street transport. For this reason also, as well as for reasons of general amenity, steam tram locomotives were usually required to emit no smoke or steam and not to exceed a certain speed, in England 8mph. Hence steam tram engines were amongst the first users of smokeless fuel and were fitted with automatic governors to apply the brake when the statutory speed was exceeded. Various devices were produced in order to avoid the visible escape of steam into the atmosphere. In the Wilkinson engine the steam was superheated to escape through the chimney, but the usual arrangement was to turn it back into water by passing it through a condensor, normally an arrangement of tubes on the roof through which the steam was passed to be cooled by the air.

One of the earliest tramways said to have used steam dummies was the San Francisco Market Street Railroad, the first in that city, which opened in July 1860. It had been intended to use horses, but the line ran through an undeveloped area of shifting sand dunes which impeded the track, making mechanical traction essential. Dummies with one or two trailers were therefore operated along Market Street to Fremont. The track was in the centre of the street but below the road surface, the resultant cutting being known after one of the directors as McCoppin's Canal. It is unlikely that the dummies described here were the enclosed condensing engines which later became typical, and steam operation was not continuous anyway. San Francisco, however, later had two steam dummy lines operating from cable termini to the beach.

The first enclosed tramway locomotives to be built in Britain were in fact an order of eight for Pernambuco in Brazil delivered by Manning, Wardle & Co from 1867. The first to be actually put into service in England was built by Henry Hughes in 1876 for experimental use on the Leicester tramways. It was not popular there and was transferred to the Vale of Clyde lines in Glasgow where a fleet of such engines operated the first urban steam tramway in Britain. This design of engine was not particularly successful though, and the Govan fleet had to be replaced within four years. A London firm, Merryweathers, produced some much more reliable engines which inaugurated the first regular steam tramway service in Europe on the Southern Tramways of Paris in March 1876. Merryweather engines were built for many other places, including Barcelona, Kassel, Guernsey, Sydney and Wellington. Other English tramway locomotive builders included Wilkinson, whose engines had a vertical boiler, and Kitson, perhaps the most successful British design, with a total production of 302.

The urban steam tramway probably had a greater vogue in the Midlands and North of England than it did in most other areas. There were about 50 undertakings at one time or another in England running over 500 locomotives, whereas in the United States, a much larger country, there were only slightly more engines—698 in 1892. There were some city lines operated in other countries, most notable amongst these being the steam tramways in Sydney, Australia and Christchurch, New Zealand. The former city had two steam tramway undertakings, both of which were very long-lived, closing respectively in 1937 and 1943. The larger of the two was operated by the New South Wales Government and had a fleet of over 100 Baldwin engines, over a fifth of the firm's entire production. Kitson engines were used on the Christchurch system, which was much smaller, but regular service lasted from 1880 to 1912, with rush hour extras until 1925. Some of the other locomotives were retained for ballast trains, and number 7 of 1881 was preserved and is now operating on a museum line.

So far as Europe was concerned steam tramways were not used very much within the towns themselves, but a vast mileage was built up in the suburbs and in the countryside. These light railways, consideration of which is referred to a later chapter, accounted for the majority of the approximately 3,000 engines constructed by continental builders, who included Krauss, Henschel, Winterthur, Breda and various Belgian firms. There were some urban lines, but these were few and far between. One of the first was at Rouen, in France, where an assortment of engines from Merryweather, a French firm and Fox, Walker & Co, another small British manufacturer, were operating in the 1880s. It was found that due to the need for repairs and alterations running costs were actually higher than for a horse line. Berlin had two or three lines run by the Berliner Dampfstrassenbahn Konsortium, one of them on the Kurfürstendam, characterised by having widely separated stopping places provided with stations. The BDK fleet included 30 Rowan steam cars as well as a number of locomotives and trailers. A very interesting line was to be found on the outskirts of Turin where, according to *Baedeker's Guide* for 1903, tourists could take a steam trram from Piazza Castello to Sassi and from thence could proceed to the royal burial church on top of the hill at Superga by cable tram. This would have been a funicular rather than a cable tram proper, but nevertheless 'no change of carriages [was necessary] in the case of "trenidiretti"'. The line is still open as an electric rack tramway. In the then capital of the Austrian Empire, Vienna, two companies operated steam trams into the country, and from 1895 one of the two urban companies, the Neue Wiener Tramway-Gesellschaft, converted some of its horse tramways to steam. One of these, from Schottenring to Nussdorf, was worked by 'mixed cars' drawn by horses in the inner city and locomotives in the suburbs. But there were few large systems in continental Europe, and few towns which relied entirely upon steam trams for their local transport.

In England the largest system under one ownership was the Manchester, Bury, Rochdale & Oldham Steam Tramways Co, which had 30 miles of route on two gauges. Huddersfield, which had 29 route miles, was thus the largest standard gauge (actually 4ft 7¾in) system, famous also for being the first tramway to be both owned and operating by a municipality. The shortest was the 1 mile 27 chain Drypool and Marfleet line in Hull, which opened in 1889 with five Milnes cars and four engines built by Thomas Green & Sons Ltd; an unusual feature was the use of two trailers. The largest concentration of steam tramways in the country was in the Black Country where several companies had independent systems. The Birmingham tramways had several interesting operational features, including the use of coloured lights at night to distinguish the routes and oil gas for lighting, this being brought to the depots in rail tank wagons. Something unique to the British steam tramways, yet common to them all, was the use of double-deck trailers. It had at first been intended to haul trains of horse cars, but the Board of Trade

Below Drypool and Marfleet steam locomotive No 1, built in 1889 by Green of Leeds, towing a massive 74-seat top-covered bogie trailer by Milnes [*Hull Daily Mail*

forbade this on street routes so, to obtain adequate capacity, double-deck trailers had to be used. For obvious reasons they were usually top covered, either fully enclosed or with a canopy, although open-top cars were retained in some places, for example in Burnley. These cars had a capacity of 60 or 70 seated on longitudinal seats below and a knifeboard seat above, the latter being replaced in some cases by garden seats.

The main advantages of steam over horse trams was that they had a higher capacity and could cope with hills far better. But the legal restrictions put upon them and the relatively small size of the locomotives, intended to save costs, meant that they were not as efficient as they might have been. And anyway steam was simply not a suitable form of power for city streets. The engines were too heavy, they were dirty, and they were rather prone to accidents. Huddersfield had a serious runaway in 1883 when seven people were killed and 28 injured, and in 1891 an engine exploded. The cost of operation, moreover, was not dramatically less than it had been with horses. Clearly steam could only be regarded as a partial success, with the exception of the rural lines to be considered later.

One way round the problems of steam traction lay in devising lighter types of prime mover, the two main possibilities here being gas or oil engines. Early experiments were carried on with ammonia gas by a Dr Emile Lamm in New Orleans in 1871. The car, which was powered by a cylinder of ammonia carried inside a reservoir of hot water on the roof, actually did run, but problems connected with the escape of gas into the atmosphere and its chemical action upon iron led to an early end of the experiment. There were actually three small tram systems in Great Britain with a fleet wholly or partly powered by town gas. These were at Lytham St Annes, where the trams ran from 1896 to 1903, Trafford Park in Manchester and Neath in South Wales. The latter, using ex-Lytham cars, carried on until 1920. The cars were open-top double-deckers seating 40 with a large flywheel on one side. They were supposed to develop 15hp, but sometimes needed a push on the railway bridges at Lytham, and were a rather slow and inefficient means of travel. Experiments took place elsewhere, for example in Croydon in 1893 and in Copenhagen in 1896, in both cases using German-built trams, and in both without result.

A very early form of internal combustion engine, fueled by naptha, powered the Conelly Motor which had trials on both sides of the Atlantic towards the end of the century. In America a converted horse car ran along the Brooklyn, Flatbush and Coney Island Street Railway in 1887, and in 1892 a car built by the British firm of Weymann of Guildford was tried at Croydon and on Rotherhithe New Road in London, where it ran for six months. However, although the motor had some advanced features like magneto ignition and a friction wheel type of infinitely variable transmission, the internal combustion engine at that time was simply not reliable enough for street railway use.

By the end of the first decade of the twentieth century, however, a relatively efficient form of petrol engine had been developed, and although most tramways had been electrified by then there were one or two special cases where internal combustion trams could be used. Some very small horse systems simply could not afford to electrify, and one or two of these motorised some of their old cars. The Stirling and Bridge of Allan Company, for example, had one double-deck car motorised by the Scottish Commercial Car Co Ltd in 1913 and operated it successfully from Stirling to St Ninians. Unfortunately the war prevented the intended conversion of the whole system, and it closed in 1920. At around the same period mechanisation of tramways in Karachi, Pakistan, was being considered. Electrification was not thought worth while, and John Abbott and John Dixon Abbott designed and built two petrol cars which entered service in 1909. These were so successful that they had entirely replaced the horses by 1912, one of the main advantages being that it was not necessary to relay the track as would normally have been the case. The system, the only one in Pakistan, is still running today, though now using open-sided cross-bench cars powered by diesel engines.

In many places there was a prejudice against overhead wires in certain streets, and in one or two cases petrol-electric trams were used to get round this problem. In Hastings, a south coast resort in England, the gap between the wires was covered by ordinary electric cars powered by a petrol-driven generator under the stairs. Three similar cars were specially built by the London County Council in 1912 for a route which was to run through the Borough of Stepney which had refused permission to erect overhead. The cars were actually used for a short while on a route in Greenwich, but were soon relegated to shunting trailers at

Marius Road depot, Balham. A diesel-electric car, however, survives in Blackpool where overhead line car 3 has a diesel motor enabling it to operate independently of the overhead supply when necessary—a useful feature in Blackpool with its many miles of railway-type track where road tower wagons cannot be used.

Petrol or diesel trams have been quite successful on rural tramways, but they have never been common on urban routes. They have occasionally been used to open new services as an inexpensive way of testing demand. Berlin ran three petrol trams over a suburban light railway between 1923 and 1929, when the line was electrified, and more recently Sapporo in Japan had a fleet of modern diesel trams built to operate an unwired extension. It also has three diesel snowbrooms. Perhaps the strangest use of petrol engines on tramways has been in cases where horse tramways, instead of mechanising their trams, have had them towed by motor cars. Several minor lines in the Netherlands did this in the 1920s, for example in Alkmaar and between Amsterdam and Sloten, and there was one example in England involving a private tramway to an isolation hospital at Dartford near London.

But 40 years before this the internal combustion engine was not a practical possibility. There was in fact no real alternative to the steam engine. However its disadvantages of danger, dirt and weight could be obviated by transmitting its power to some lighter vehicle in the street. There were a number of ways of doing this, some of which worked and some which did not, but which all seemed worth exploring at the time. One of the simpler alternatives was the fireless steam locomotive in which the boiler and the firebox were replaced by an insulated tank containing superheated water under high pressure, the tank being recharged at termini from a stationary boiler. The same Dr Lamm who designed an ammonia-driven tram built one of these locomotives for the New Orleans and Carrolton tramway in 1875. Cars were hauled by mule to the city boundary where the new steam engines took over. M Leon Francq of Paris built an improved version which ran for many years on the rural tramway from Rueil to Marly-le-Roi, but such engines found no general acceptance for tramway use.

A rather similar idea was to drive the engines not by steam but by compressed air, storage tanks on the car being charged when necessary from steam-driven compressors built at strategic intervals along the route. A dummy locomotive was built by Greenwood and Batley in Great Britain to the design of a Major Beaumont in 1877 for trials in Woolwich, and an improved version ran in 1881 on the North Metropolitan line between Leytonstone and Stratford. The tanks were recharged by a hose connected to an airline via a manhole in the road. The Beaumont engine was driven by highly compressed air, but it was soon found that that caused so many problems—such as overheated compressors, excessively heavy equipment, and the risk of explosion— that it proved impracticable. An alternative design using air at a lower pressure proved more viable. Such a car was used experimentally in Cincinnatti in 1885, and a few years later a fleet of air cars ran for nearly two years in Rome, New York. But the only compressed air tram to have even a limited commercial value was the Mekarski car in France. The inventor patented his compressed air engine in 1872, and by 1876 an experimental car was being tried on the Courbevoi line of the Tramway Nord in Paris. This car was a single-decker with 20 seats plus 14 standing places on the rear platform. There were two plate iron reservoirs underneath the car, one main and one reserve, and the air was warmed by hot water or steam before use. The engine worked well, and by 1879 the tramway system of Nantes was being operated by a fleet of these cars, in this case seating nineteen with twelve on the platform. The first line to be opened was $3\frac{3}{4}$ miles long with 10 compressor stations, at which cars took 20 minutes to be charged for one trip at the rather low average speed of $5\frac{1}{2}$mph. The fleet later totalled 22 single-deck and four double-deck cars, and the system was not electrified until 1913. Most of the Mekarski cars worked in Paris, where the first were introduced at Nogent-sur-Marne in 1887. The fleet of large double-deckers eventually totalled 208, and as late as 1910 there were half-a-dozen routes in operation, the last cars not being withdrawn until 1914. In the United Kingdom the British Mekarski Improved Air Engine Co Ltd experimented with a car designed by Sir Frederick Bramwell in 1883 in London, but the nearest approach to a regular service came in 1885 when from 28 February to 16 June five 38 seat cars built by the Lancaster Wagon Co with engines by Clayton and Co of Preston ran from Kings Cross to Holloway Road.

Another attempt to use steam power indirectly was a complete failure. In this system a steam engine was used to wind clockwork springs fitted in barrels on the tram. A Philadelphia company was engaged in

designing a car with eighty springs in the early 1880s, it being expected
that it could run up to 8 miles between windings, but it does not appear
that any such car ever ran in the United States. However in Britain a
tractive unit was patented by E. H. Leveaux, a Belgian, and one was actually built in 1874. In the following year it was demonstrated hauling a
passenger car in the Lillie Bridge depot of the Metropolitan District
Railway, when it ran at 7mph for $\frac{1}{2}$ mile on one winding of its six springs.
By 1876 24 springs were capable of taking it up to 2 miles, but this is the
last time we hear of the car.

The only really serious opposition to steam trams in the pre-electric
era was the cable tramway which enjoyed some considerable success,
especially in the United States and Australasia. Even in America there
were more steam undertakings than there were cable, but the latter were
amongst the largest and most important in the country with over ten
times as many trams running in the 1890s. At that time the average length
of the individual cable systems was longer than that for any other form of
traction, even including electricity, which by then had come to be used
on almost 90 per cent of American tramways. The principle of the cable
tramway was quite simple. A stationary steam engine kept a cable
moving continuously in a slot under the street. Trams were controlled
by attaching them to or detaching them from this cable at will. However
simple the idea was in theory, though, the practical difficulties were
immense. For example, some foolproof method of gripping and releas-
ing the cable was needed, whilst the channel in which the cable travelled
had to be wide enough for the cable-car mechanism yet narrow enough
to avoid causing any obstruction to other road traffic. Various inventors
put their minds to the solution of these problems, and in fact W. J.
Curtis, the English tramway pioneer, patented a quick-release gripper as
early as 1838, whilst the essentials of the system were suggested by E. S.
Gardiner of Philadelphia. However, despite this theoretical work, and
despite the fact that cable haulage had long been used in mines and quar-
ries, all the credit for producing a workable cable tramway must go to
Andrew S. Hallidie, the promoter and designer of the first line in San
Francisco. Hallidie was in fact a manufacturer of wire ropes, so he was in
some sense self-interested.

Within a year he had worked out the basic principles of a cable
tramway and had surveyed California Street with a view to laying a line.

This scheme fell through, however, and a franchise was obtained for a line along Clay Street. It proved very difficult to convince others of the scheme's merits and to obtain financial backing, but eventually Hallidie and three friends, backed by a bank, were able to start work in May 1872.

The Clay Street Hill line, in common with other early cable tramways, was operated by two-car trains consisting of a dummy or grip car and a passenger trailer. The grip car was open at the sides and the driver, known as the gripman, stood in the middle. Seats were usually provided at the front and the sides for passengers, with others in the covered trailer behind. It was believed that the steep hills would make long or heavy cars impracticable. The cable, running in a small tunnel between the tracks, was attached to the car by a device known as the grip. This consisted of a long rod which passed through the slot in the road and which could be turned by a wheel on the car to bring the faces of the gripper into contact with the rope. Hallidie's pioneer line soon became a commercial success, and he himself made a great deal of money from the use of his patents on the other lines which began to spring up before the end of the decade.

The cable itself actually consisted of a manilla hemp heart bound with six strands of steel, each made up of 16 or more wires, the whole being capable of about twice the load expected of it. When a new cable was fitted, which was necessary at between four months and a year, it had to be rolled out through the streets and then hand-spliced. Splicing was also necessary several times during the cable's life due to stretching and whenever the cable became worn or a strand broke—mechanical strand alarms gave warning of any such weakness. The cable ran in a tunnel under the road surface, this normally being lined either with concrete or with brick. The slot itself was made of metal supported at frequent intervals by horseshoe shaped cast iron yokes. Apart from the necessity of supporting the weight of other road traffic, the main problem was extremes of heat and cold which caused the slot to expand or contract. Difficulties such as these caused the first car in Pittsburgh to take a week to complete a run which should have taken one hour. However the yokes were redesigned to take account of these defects, and by the mid-1880s cable car track was extremely robust and reliable.

San Francisco itself probably had more competing cable lines than anywhere else, for by 1889 there were eight of them. The third of these to be built, the California Street, was the most luxurious ever constructed when it was opened in 1878. Twenty five cable cars and dummies were brought, about half built by the Kimball Manufacturing Company of San Francisco and the rest by the Central Pacific shops at Sacramento, their livery being a striking maroon and gold. This company introduced a new form of grip operated by a lever rather than a wheel. Throwing the lever forward released the cable to run free through the jaws of the grip, whilst it could be tightened gradually to accelerate the car by degrees. The cars had three separate braking systems, or four if one counts the cable itself, which naturally restricted the car to its own speed. Normal brake shoes operating on the wheels were provided, supplemented by track brakes made of large blocks of soft pine, and, for emergency use only, a tapered piece of metal which could be jammed into the slot to bring the car to an immediate halt. Another later innovation was the California car which did away with the separate dummy. The cars used today on the California Street line are double ended, with a closed centre saloon and an open grip section at either end, which means that turntables are not needed. The other surviving San Francisco lines along Powell Street also use California cars, but theirs are single ended and need turntables at each terminus and in the car-barn where it replaces pointwork. Some cars with fully-enclosed saloons were built for other systems, the driver operating the grip from an open platform, just like the driver of an electric trolley. One American example was in Cincinnatti, but enclosed cars like this, with the addition of an upper deck, were much more common in the United Kingdom than elsewhere.

The most important system in San Francisco was the Market Street Cable Railway which operated five separate routes distinguished in horse-tram style by different coloured cars. Most other cable tramway undertakings later amalgamated with the Market Street company, which became known as the United Railroads from 1902 to 1921, when, as a result of a financial collapse, the old name was resumed until the Municipal Railway took over in 1944. The California Street company was not taken over until as late as 1952.

San Francisco's pre-eminent place in the past and present of the cable car has tended to overshadow the fact that many other cities and towns

Above A modern view of a San Francisco California-type cable car on the Bay-Taylor turntable [*San Francisco Municipal Railway*

had extensive systems. There were in fact 62 cable tramways in the United States, and all the major cities except Atlanta, Boston, Detroit and New Orleans had cable cars at one time or another. Chicago had the largest system in the world, Kansas City the third largest, whilst two of the most important lines in New York, the Broadway and the Third Avenue, operated 47 miles of route by cable. Others were much smaller affairs, like the San Diego Cable Railway opened in 1890 with only 12 cars built by the rather unlikely Stockton Combine, Harvester and Agricultural Works. Its cars all had Spanish style names like *Montezuma* and *San Ysidora*. Los Angeles had three cable lines, including the Pacific Railway Company which opened 10½ miles of route in 1889.

True cable tramways were an Anglo-Saxon phenomena, being found only in the United States, Australasia and the United Kingdom. The first cable tramway in Europe was opened by the Steep Grade Tramways and Works Co Ltd, a subsidiary of Hallidie's European company. The 3ft 6in gauge line up Highgate Hill was intended more for exhibition purposes than for any traffic potential, which was fortunate, because the cars were rarely filled, and by 1889 both the parent and the operating companies had gone into liquidation. The line carried on under new management for three years, but then an accident caused its closure for five years, and it was finally replaced in 1909. The only other cable tramway in London had an even shorter life of less than fifteen years. In the early 1890s the London Tramways Co extended their existing horse line by cable up Brixton Hill to Streatham, and from December 1892 the section between Kennington and Brixton was turned over to cable too. In 1895 the line was extended to Streatham library. The main depot was at Telford Avenue, with a smaller one for grip cars on Brixton Road. Ordinary horse cars were used as trailers, and these ran through to the Westminster and Blackfriars Bridges. After the London County Council took over it put grippers on the cars themselves, and after electrification two four wheel cars were fitted with grippers which could be interchanged with the conduit plough. An experimental through service was operated between August and October 1903, but it was not a success, and the cable line closed in April 1904.

Neither of these lines augured well for the success of cable traction in the United Kingdom, and indeed there were only four others, in Birmingham, Douglas, Matlock and Edinburgh, all except the last being small, one route systems. The Scottish capital, however, had one of the largest systems in the world, and probably the most complex of any. This was partly because instead of being a series of competing and separate lines, as in San Francisco, with the exception of two earlier routes it was planned as a whole with numerous junctions and with provision for through running from one part of the city to the other. Also the city council insisted that these junctions should be worked without resort to gravity operation, which meant that auxiliary cables had to be installed to provide 'power' for the curves between main cables. The engineer to the tramways, which were owned by the corporation and let to a company, invented a new type of grip to cope with these complicated requirements. The cars, which were mostly normal British open-top double-deckers, had a grip fitted to each platform. These had jaws on either side worked by a wheel and shaft on a fixed pillar, and a lever on the pillar made it possible to change from one grip to the other at will. So one cable could be dropped on the right and another picked up on the left, whilst where a cable ran underneath another at a junction it could be dropped at the front, the car taken over the junction by the rear gripper, and then the cable picked up again by the front gripper.

The first two routes were opened by the Edinburgh Northern Company in 1888 and 1890, and it was their success which persuaded the corporation to adopt a similar system on the recently acquired horse tramway network. The first route was not actually opened until late in 1899, by which time the success of electric traction elsewhere was assured. However overhead wires were simply not acceptable in Edinburgh then, and the conversion was virtually complete by 1902, although some extensions were made as late as 1908. There were four power stations, at Henderson Row (ex-Northern), Portobello, Shrubhill and Tollcross. The complexities of operation were enormous. The first route between Pilrig and Braid Hills, for example, required three main cables and three auxiliaries, the latter to provide access to Shrubhill depot and to cover the last section of the route to Pilrig, for St Andrew's junction, and for access to Tollcross depot. Auxiliary cables were driven at half speed from one of the main cable diverting pulleys, and normally arranged to cross above the main cables. In cases like this where it was necessary to disconnect the gripper a safety device known as a pawl was provided. If the car did not release the cable in time the cable was pulled out of place and bore against a lever which barred the gripper's path and brought the car to a sudden halt. San Francisco has a rather less drastic device which pulls the cable out of the grip. Drivers were assisted to observe the cable-changing operations by an elaborate system of road markings of squares, circles and other shapes, but even so considerable difficulty was caused by the complexity of the system. There were several cases of cars hitting the pawls, often with serious results. Matters came to a head in 1902 when the company refused to pay its rental, claiming that the system was unworkable. As a result various improvements were made then and in later years which made it possible to remove some of the auxiliaries and pawls and to dispense with rear gripper operation. The greatest bone of contention, the circular service, was finally abandoned in 1906, and from then on the system operated quite satisfactorily for a long period. At around the same time top covers began to be fitted to the cars, which were all bogie vehicles, and oil lighting was replaced by acetylene.

Australia and New Zealand were the only other countries to have cable tramways. Dunedin's closed as recently as 1956, and Sydney also ran cable cars from 1884 to 1905. But the largest system in this area was in Melbourne where tramway service was inaugurated by cable in 1885. Normally cable tramways replaced earlier horse tramways, but Melbourne was unusual in never having more than a few isolated horse lines. A total of 15 routes were constructed up to 1891, when the maximum of $43\frac{3}{4}$ route miles of double track was reached. Grip cars and four wheel trailers were used, the first 20 units being imported from the United States and the remainder of the sets being built locally. Each route had its own fleet of cars, painted in distinctive colours, and lettered with their destinations. From 1916 the system, which had been leased to a company, was taken over by a public authority, from 1920 known as the Melbourne and Metropolitan Tramways Board. At that time there were 46 miles of cable track, which included the formerly independent Northcote Tramway, and about 450 tram sets. Although it was soon decided to work towards complete electrification, this was a long term process where so large a system was concerned, and in fact some 150 new cable car sets were built up to 1924 to alleviate the shortage of rolling stock. By 1929 only 15 route miles had been electrified, and it was not until 26 October 1940 that the last cable tram ran on the Bourke Street route.

The Melbourne cable tramway system in fact survived far longer than most. In the United States there was a rapid decline in cable mileage around the turn of the century, for although cable tramways were cheap to operate they were extremely expensive to build, which made it uneconomic to extend them into the outer suburbs which the new electric lines were tapping. New overhead electric systems replaced cables in places such as Philadelphia and Baltimore before the end of the nineteenth century, and the two major lines in New York were being converted to the conduit system at the same time. Chicago's last car ran in 1906, and in the same year San Francisco's Sutter Street system was largely replaced by electricity as a result of the disastorous fire and earthquake. The California Street system was almost completely destroyed. The president of the company, J. B. Stetson, described how the earthquake damaged the power house and cut off the water supply, so that when fire broke out 'every car in the house and those on the street, some of them eight blocks away, fifty-two in all—were burned except one',

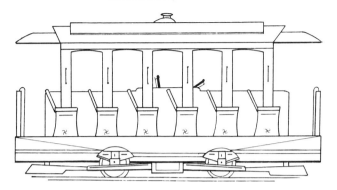

An open grip car of the Cleveland City Cable Railway [*P. N. C. Cooke*

whilst the engine house was seriously damaged and 'the tracks and slot rail . . . were badly bent and twisted in many places'. However service was resumed in August 1906 with four cars in a priming coat of paint and part of the line is still running today. This was an isolated case, however, and apart from San Francisco, Seattle and Tacoma few American systems survived long into the twentieth century. In the United Kingdom the Edinburgh system, which had deteriorated considerably during the war,

Below   Melbourne's first cable grip car and trailer were built in 1885 and remained in service until the system closed in 1940   [*Melbourne Metropolitan Tramways Board*

was converted very quickly between 1921 and 1923, whilst the Matlock and Douglas lines were closed respectively in 1927 and 1929.

Today the only surviving cable tramways are those in San Francisco, where they operate as an officially designated national historic landmark, probably the only mobile landmarks in the world! There are one or two other lines operated by cable, like the Great Orme Tramway in Wales, but these are not true cable tramways, but funiculars, with one car permanently attached to each end of a non-continuous cable. San Francisco itself once had one such line up the incredible 1 in 3.5 Telegraph Hill, but it was not a success. The Great Orme line is operated in two independent sections, with two cars on each, and the lower section which runs through the street gives a very good impression of what a cable tramway was like.

CHAPTER THREE

THE EARLY ELECTRIC TRAMCAR

MOST of the basic principles of electro-magnetism had been discovered by the early part of the nineteenth century, but pioneer inventors who tried to apply this knowledge to the field of transport were hampered by the fact that the only source of energy to hand was the primary zinc-fueled battery. Apart from being an extremely costly way to produce electricity, the amount of current available was simply not enough to power a vehicle for any length of time or at a commercial speed. Nevertheless some quite serious attempts were made to do this, beginning with Thomas Davenport, a New England blacksmith, who exhibited a model electric railway in 1835, this being closely followed by Robert Davidson's full-scale locomotive which ran occasionally on Scottish metals before being destroyed by an angry crowd of steam railway men. Both these locomotives obtained their power from batteries carried on the car, as did that of Professor Charles G. Page, which resembled nothing more than an early beam engine, with its long cranks, its fly-wheel, and its hollow magnets which replaced steam cylinders. One version of this design actually attained 19 mph on a test run near Washington in 1851, but the United States Government was not impressed with the way in which the batteries dissolved into clouds of choking acid fumes after their supreme effort, and the authorities refused to provide further funds. Another American, Professor Farmer, had a rather better idea about the same time when he built a model electric vehicle which obtained its current from lineside batteries connected to the rails; but of course there was still no more power available. There seems to have been a pause in experimentation after these disappointing results, although as late as 1875 a mechanic named George F. Green was trying out his own design of battery-powered car in his home town in Michigan, interestingly enough using the later almost universal system of power supply via an overhead line with the return circuit through the rails. But Green was aware that for his invention to be successful he would have to use a dynamo. These had been developed during the 1860s, and in 1870 the first really effective generator was built by the Belgian-born Frenchman Z. T. Gramme, who in 1872 made the interesting discovery that if a dynamo was fed electricity it acted as a motor, and it was with such reversed dynamos that the first electric locomotives were powered. However the early electrical pioneers tended to concentrate on the possibilities of electric lighting to the exclusion of traction, and it was not until 1879 that the world's first practicable electric locomotive was built.

This locomotive, built by Werner von Siemens and powered by a 2 hp dynamo, was demonstrated at the Berlin Industrial Exhibition of 1879 on a 300m circuit of narrow gauge track. Current was picked up from a central third rail, and small though it was the locomotive could haul three trailers seating 18 passengers at 7km/h, a total of 80,000 people being carried over the duration of the exhibition. This was the first time that an electric locomotive had performed so reliably, although it was not long before others were seeking to emulate this success. Other experiments which involved the use of locomotive haulage included those begun by Edison at Menlo Park in the United States only a year later. Although the control and braking systems on his locomotive were rather unsophisticated, consisting respectively of an on-off switch and two wooden blocks, its 10hp converted dynamo could take it to speeds of up to 40mph. Also in the United States an expatriate Englishman, Leo Daft, built a very neat locomotive named the *Ampere*, which in 1883 was demonstrated hauling a carriage along a narrow gauge railway in New York State. Unfortunately it came off the rails and was wrecked on the return trip, but this did not dampen the enthusiasm of Daft, who played a considerable part in the early development of the electric streetcar. Meanwhile Siemens had been exhibiting his system at various places, including the International Electric Exhibition held at the Crystal Palace, London, in 1881–2. In the latter year a second line was operating at the Palace, this time built by Henry Bock Binko, a man almost entirely unknown until unearthed by the researches of A. Winston Bond and published in *Modern Tramway* Nos 340/1. His line was comparable to that of Siemens in most respects, apart from the two-rail current supply and the rather higher speed and capacity claimed for it. This line seems to have closed in 1884, but in the same year the equipment was transported to the Forestry Exhibition in Edinburgh, where Binko's International Electric Railway gained fame by transporting, on two memorable occasions, both the Prince and Princess of Wales and the Prime Minister and Mrs Gladstone, a specially-built carriage being procured for the purpose.

While all this experimental work was going on, Siemens had opened the world's first electric tramway to offer a public service. His firm, Siemens & Halske (S&H), had built a metre gauge tramway along the course of a derelict railway line between Gross-Lichterfelde station and the nearby military Cadet School in the Berlin suburbs, a distance of 2.5km (1½ miles). An experimental run was made on 12 May 1881 and the line was opened to the public on 16 May, although for many years afterwards it was used basically for experimental purposes with only a limited public service, which in 1883, for example, amounted to only 12 journeys a day. There may have have been one or two cars—certainly there were two by 1883—and these were converted horse trams seating 26 passengers and powered by a 5.5hp reversed dynamo fitted under the floor and driving both axles by means of 13.5mm wire ropes specially imported from Hungary. By 1889 there were three cars, on one of which the steel coils had been replaced by a fully-enclosed chain drive. The current was controlled by the later generally adopted system of resistances and notched controllers, although other designers were to follow numerous dead ends before they reached similar conclusions. The highest permitted speed was 20km/h, but the car was said to be capable of more than twice this velocity. The 180v current was fed directly through the running rails, a system which resulted in considerable problems, for although the Lichterfelde line was fenced this did not stop horses receiving shocks at road crossings, and nor did it stop the curious from dismantling the fence and using it to short-circuit the rails, which were anyway subject to considerable leakage of current. The voltage was cut to 100 to try and reduce the public nuisance, but even so it was quite obvious that such a system could never be applied to street tramways.

Above The side-conductor rail is clearly shown in this dramatic view of a Portrush electric car at Dunluce Castle, Co Antrim [*Ulster Museum*

Since it took a number of years to devise a safe and effective alternative method of current collection, most of the successful electric lines which were built in the 1880s used variants of the rail conductor system, and were therefore usually on their own rights of way. A number of these lines were to be found in the United Kingdom, where some of the first practical attempts to turn electricity to commercial advantage in the field of transport were made. A line with several firsts to its credit was that built by the Traill brothers between Portrush and Bushmills in what is now Northern Ireland. This was one of the first electric railways in the world, and the first to operate tramcars by electricity in the United Kingdom. It was also the first to use water as a source of power, although this occasioned some debate until it was decided that the fish would not be injured by the current! And it was almost certainly the first line upon which an electric tramcar was driven by a woman, Miss Jeannie Richardson, who was deputed by Mr William Traill to take charge of the car on the official opening run on 28 September 1883. On that day the line was opened by Earl Spencer, the Lord Lieutenant of Ireland, and, according to an observer, 'Vast numbers of people congregated at both ends of the system and along the entire coast road and were amazed to witness tramcars moving steadily and slowly along without visible means of propulsion'. As a matter of fact the official opening date was not very significant, for electric cars had been running intermittently from at least the April of that year, and they continued to run intermittently for many years afterwards. For most of its length the line ran on a slightly raised pavement on the seaward side of the coast road to Bushmills, and from 1887 a further extension went across country from there to the famous Giant's Causeway. This layout made it possible to use third rail current collection, the rail in this case being mounted on 17in high wooden posts along the seaward side of the line. The rail was interrupted to provide access to fields etc, and only one track was provided with a conductor at loops, downhill cars having to coast through. It was only possible to board carriages from the landward side, and the last $\frac{1}{2}$ mile through the streets of Portrush had to be operated by steam tram engines, which was a fortunate circumstance, as they were needed to maintain a major part of the service for many years. As late as 1887 steam mileage amounted to 17,797 and electric to only 4,721, but from 1899, when overhead wires were installed, steam began to be eliminated. The electrical equipment was by Siemens, who were involved in the vast majority of early European installations, although the cars were by British builders. The line was entirely dependent upon tourist traffic, and its last season was in 1949, when it closed after a chequered but distinguished career.

Another line which became and remains a tourist attraction is Volks Railway along the seafront at Brighton. Magnus Volk, of German extraction, was a very inventive man, who amongst other things provided electric lighting for the Brighton Pavilion. In 1883 he obtained permission from Brighton Corporation to lay a short electric railway along the beach. Its gauge was 2ft, the current, which was derived from the obligatory Siemens dynamo, was fed into the running rails, and a small double-ended car was specially made by a local builder. The railway was opened on 4 August 1883 and a regular service was offered until the end of the year. Volk then obtained permission to lay a more permanent line which opened on 4 April 1884, and which ran a regular 5–6 min service from then until 1940, apart from the occasional closure because of gale damage. The gauge was increased to 2ft 9in, later reduced to 2ft 8½in, and two new cars equipped with 10hp Siemens dynamos were acquired to work the $\frac{3}{4}$-mile line. Later on a third rail was provided, and a further extension was made in 1901, by which time most of the track was supported by timber or steel viaducts to minimise gale damage. A total of 13 cars, all except one fully or partially open, have been used on the line, of which nine remain, two of them being secondhand from the Southend Pier Tramway, another early line which was opened in 1890. Piers of course provided one place where rail-fed electrified lines could work safely, and the pioneer horse line along Ryde Pier was provided with a third rail electric tramway by Siemens in 1886, which worked until replaced by petrol trams in 1927. Volk managed to find another place where electric lines could operate 'safely'—in the sea! His Brighton and Rottingdean Seashore Electric Tramroad consisted of a sort of mobile pier which ran on two parallel tracks on the seabed between 1896 and 1901.

Another pioneer line, again in Ireland and again supplied with current by means of hydro-electric power, almost a necessity in remote areas before electricity became generally available, was the three mile tramway between Newry station and a flax mill at Bessbrook. Built under the direction of Dr Edward Hopkinson, a man often met with as consultant to early electric lines in Great Britain, it was opened on 10 September 1885 using the third rail method of current collection. However where the line crossed a road at Millvale an overhead wire replaced the third rail, and cars were fitted with a pick-up consisting of a contact strip on a large metal frame, an early form of bow collector, this being the first recorded use of overhead current collection in the United Kingdom. Another interesting feature was the two additional rails set outside and just below the 3ft gauge track, these being used by specially built wagons which could be drawn by horses on the road and by electric car on the tramway, this again being one of the first known examples of such a technique. Two motor cars, built by the Ashbury Wagon Co Ltd, were provided for the opening, one being smaller than the other. Both were bogie cars, and the single Hopkinson motor drove the rear axle of the leading bogie via a chain, the wheels of the bogie being coupled by connecting rods. One Starbuck trailer was also provided, together with 24 carts, and some further secondhand acquisitions were made before the line closed in 1948. Its historical importance was immense, for its success influenced the directors of the City and South London Railway to employ electricity on what became the world's first underground electric railway.

Another little line was opened in 1886 at Carstairs House near Glasgow, this being the first permanent electric tramway in Scotland, although it was only for the private use of the owners of the house. It ran from the nearby railway station for the carriage of both passengers and goods, its current, again derived from water power, being supplied via positive and negative wires carried on posts at the side of the track. Two years earlier, though, an electric tram had actually run in the streets of Edinburgh, the inspiration behind it being, once again, Henry Bock Binko. He fitted the electrical equipment from his exhibition railway into an ordinary horse car, which he then gained permission to run for about 700yd from the Exhibition gate to the Haymarket Railway Station, and a fairly successful demonstration took place on 11 October 1884. Binko's system was quite unsuitable for general use on street tramways, as he picked up the current by means of a wheeled collector running along two lines of copper plate laid between the tracks. But nontheless he had succeeded in running the first street tramcar in the United Kingdom to be supplied with electricity from a stationary source, as opposed to accumulator cars which were self-contained.

Progress was also being made in the United States, where in 1885 Leo Daft electrified a horse tramway branch in Baltimore, using locomotives on the third rail system. The three-mile branch to Hampden was a very hilly one, and, thus it provided a fair test for electric traction, which was a qualified success. The major problem, which caused the line to revert to horses later in the eighties, was the use of the third rail which involved excessive loss of current, sometimes so much during heavy rain that there was no power at all. And of course animals suffered electric shocks, a problem which was partially obviated by the provision of a primitive type of overhead at road crossings. This consisted of lengths of gas pipe from which current was picked up by means of a long pole which was wound up from the car.

If nothing else, these early electric lines revealed the problems which would have to be solved before widespread electrification of tramways became possible. These technical problems included how to control the flow of current to the motors, how to decrease wear on the motor caused by repeated starting, and how to position the motors so that they and the transmission to the wheels, which was another problem, would be least disturbed by the jolting of the vehicle. All these difficulties were shared with the designers of electric railways, but a problem that was specific to electric tramways was how safely to feed the current to a moving vehicle, given that the use of the rails was not possible. It is with the various solutions to this question that the rest of this chapter is concerned.

Before any effective method of power supply had been devised many tramways companies experimented with self-contained accumulator-driven cars. Some of the earliest experiments took place in Paris where battery tramcars worked a considerable mileage for a number of years, and overall accumulators had a greater vogue on the continent of Europe than they did anywhere else. Numerous tests took place, for example in Brussels, where a mile-long line in the Rue de la Loi was equipped with modified horse cars on the system of M Edmond Julien. They were equipped with no less than 120 accumulators, one motor and chain-type transmission. A full charge could take them 35km (22 miles) at a maximum speed of 12km/h on the flat. This experiment lasted only four years, as did that in Frankfurt where a short line between the Hauptbahnhof and Gallaswarte was operated by the Pollak Company. There the batteries were recharged after each journey via an attachment on the roof which clipped onto an overhead standard rather like a railway loading gauge. No more long-lived, but on a rather larger scale, was the Norrebrogade route of the Norrebros Elektriske Sporvei in Copenhagen, which opened in 1897 with 18 single-deck cars equipped by S&H. Five double-deckers were added to the fleet in 1900, but all were converted to overhead trolley operation in the following year, though not before the line had proved that electric traction was a feasible possibility in the city. Similar experiments took place in the United Kingdom, where the very first electric street tram was an accumulator car which ran at Leytonstone in London on 4 March 1882. There were numerous other trials in the capital, including one at Gunnersbury in 1883 which ended rather ignominiously with the car being hauled away by a team of horses. The same designer, Anthony Reckenzaun, later went to America where his improved battery car ran for nine months in Philadelphia. Another early British experiment took place near Brighton in the mid-eighties where the exceptionally high speed of 20mph was claimed. The most extensive trial in London was that carried out by the North Metropolitan between 1889 and 1893 when five 52-seat cars ran between Greengate and Canning Town, but accumulator traction never had any commercial importance in the United Kingdom, with the possible exception of the Bristol Road line in Birmingham which ran with 10 cars from 1890 to 1901. Experience in the rest of the world was generally similar, although some lightweight battery cars were running in New York as late as 1933. The major disadvantages of battery trams were the excessive weight of the lead-acid accumulators, the offensive fumes which they gave off—they were normally mounted under the seats—and the inability of the cars to go any distance at any speed. However it must not be forgotten that accumulator cars were often the first to run in many places, and that they performed a valuable pioneering function in awakening tramway managements to the possibilities of electric traction.

For any large-scale electrification, however, a stationary source of supply was essential, and this meant designing some form of current collector. The first one to work at all effectively was invented by Werner von Siemens and exhibited by him at the Paris Industrial Exhibition of 1881. It consisted of two slotted tubes, positive and negative, in which ran two sliding shuttles which were connected to the car by flexible cables. The Paris line operated between the Place de la Concorde and the Palais de l'Industrie using an open-top double-decker with the overhead mounted above and slightly to one side of the car. In the following year Siemens opened a second line in Berlin with a form of double wire overhead, but this proved ineffective and was almost certainly replaced by slotted tubes before the end of the year. Three permanent lines were later equipped with the same system—at Mödling, near Vienna, in 1883, at Frankfurt-am-Main in 1884, and at Montreux in 1888 and each of them retained the copper tube overhead until the early years of the twentieth century. The longest-lived was the line between Frankfurt and Offenbach which was not converted to a more conventional system until 1905–6. It was metre gauge like the others, was 6.7km long, and was single track throughout apart from the passing loops. Single-deck cars were used—the Montreux line was uncommon in having 12 double-deckers—which meant that the tubes could be suspended immediately above the track, where it looked rather like a form of catenary. The fleet eventually consisted of a total of 10 motors and 6 trailers in a dark green livery fitted, uncommonly for the period, with transverse seats. To avoid the possibility of current leaking into the rails the wheels were made out of wood with iron rims. The 15hp motors allowed a top speed of 18km/h on level stretches, the journey time being about 25min, a third of the time a horse tram would have needed. These relatively high speeds over the lightly built track earned for the line the nickname 'boneshaker', and on 13 January 1905 the local authorities purchased the Frankfurter-Offenbacher Trambahn Gesellschaft for conversion into a standard gauge line, through service being resumed on 29 October 1906. This brought to an end the last 'tube' tramway, a system which was both expensive and difficult to arrange at junctions, but which had the great merit of working, which many experimental systems did not.

Another early overhead system which was used much more widely in fact worked rather less well. This involved the use of two overhead wires upon which ran an arrangement of two or more grooved wheels which became known as a troller. It was this system which Siemens had used and rejected on his second Berlin line in Charlottenburg in 1882, and further experiments with the troller were largely if not entirely confined to North America, where many early lines were equipped in this fashion. The first person to design such a wheeled current collector in the United States seems to have been Dr Joseph R. Finney, a Pittsburg dentist, although his original intention was to use it for a railway telegraph. His traveller, as he called it, actually ran on a single wire and was first designed with two wheels on top and two wheels underneath the wire, although in a later version he used two wheels only running along the top. In August 1882 Finney operated a converted horse car in a depot yard in Allegheny, Pa., but no commercial application resulted from this first venture. In 1884, however, a farmer turned telegraph operator named John C. Henry began experimenting with a converted mule car in Kansas City. His first efforts were disastrous as he did not know how to control the speed of the motor, but eventually he designed a clutch and gear box which had the desired effect. He used double copper wires for the overhead upon which ran little two-wheeled trollers towed along by cables connected to the car, a total of four cars being equipped in this way. The line gave an intermittent service for some months, but eventually slid into bankruptcy and was replaced by a cable route.

Despite this setback other inventors with rather more technical expertise than Henry continued to champion the troller. Leo Daft, whom we have met before, opened a number of lines in Connecticut together with the Sea Shore Electric Railway in Ashbury Park, New Jersey. In this latter case the trollers had four wheels and ran upon the usual two wires, one of which was positive and the other negative. Being a tourist line, the cars were open-sided with striped blinds to unfurl in case of rain. Knowing the proclivities of Daft cars, the passengers were as likely to see falling trollers as falling rain for the great disadvantage of all trollers was the difficulty in persuading them to stay on the wires! Another early pioneer was the Belgian-born Charles Van Deopole who opened his first commercial line in South Bend in 1885 using trollers, or travellers as he called them. A number of other Van Deopole lines were opened during the next few years, including one between St. Catherines and Thorold in Ontario in 1887, the first electric tramway in Canada and also, as part of the local interurban, one of the last. Van Deopole used water power wherever he could, like the Irish lines described above, and he also believed in mounting his motors on the platform where they could be supervised. There was quite a controversy between him and Daft, who put his under the floor, on this point!

Two of the most interesting troller-equipped lines were opened in the Pittsburgh area in 1887–8. One of these, the Pittsburgh, Knoxville and St. Clair Street Railway, was electrified on the Daft system using five small locomotives towing passenger trailers on the same lines as his Baltimore route of 1885. The conditions were much more severe, however, involving gradients as steep as 15 per cent, and toothed rack rails were laid on these sections to couple with a cogwheel on the locomotive. The first 10 per cent of the line was laid with conduit current collection for some reason, but the remainder had double-wire overhead. The other line, the Observatory Hill Passenger Railway, was built in Allegheny City, then outside Pittsburgh, on the system of two other early pioneers, Bentley and Knight. It too had a conduit and a troller equipped section, together with a rack on the steepest parts of the line. The trollers were unplugged when cars left the overhead equipped section and then fixed onto the next 'up' cars. Both lines ran experimentally in 1887 and opened for public service in 1888, but by then their operating methods were already out of date.

Since the use of overhead wires was proving so unfruitful, and as a natural derivative from third rail systems, the thoughts of some inventors turned towards the idea of picking up the current from an underground source. This meant putting the wires into an underground channel, which became known as a conduit, into which some sort of collector could be introduced. Van Deopole had exhibited little conduit-fed railways in 1883 and 1884 at the Chicago and Toronto Expositions, but after that he returned to the use of the overhead wire. The first attempt to use a conduit on a street tramway was by Bentley and Knight, who took over a mile and a half of horse tramway in Cleveland, Ohio, in 1883. Their conduit was built of wooden planks to which were bolted the insulators which supported the conductor rails. It was originally intended to keep mud out of the slot by a hinged cover which the current collector would have turned open as the car passed, an idea which gave the collector the name it bore thereafter, the 'plough'. The motor, a converted dynamo, was put underneath the car where it drove the axles via wire ropes. Unfortunately both track and conduit were too lightly built, which caused frequent derailments and plough breakages, and although a fitful service was operated in 1884 the horses were back by the following year. The Bentley-Knight Company's most ambitious attempt to build and operate a conduit line took place in 1888–9 when a section of the West End Street Railway in Boston was electrified on their system. This was the first occasion in which a major company in the United States had electrified a part of its network, but after six months of almost continuous trouble the experiment was abandoned, due mainly to the fact that the conduit had not been built in a robust enough fashion.

Another conduit line several miles long was laid in Denver, Colorado, in 1886 following an experimental installation in the previous year. This line was built on the very complicated series system by Professor Sydney Short, and it closed again in less than a year. Another series—as opposed to normal parallel—conduit line was opened in Northfleet, Kent in 1889, this being the first electric tramway to be built in the London area, but again it was short-lived, closing in 1890. Professor Short also equipped one or two other American lines with overhead wires and trollers, but soon gave up his system, which involved wiring trams in series like fairy lights, and then solving the unnecessary complication of keeping the rest on the move when one had stopped.

It was in fact in England that the world's first successful conduit line, and, apart from Siemen's shuttle lines, the world's first practical electric street tramway was opened in 1885. This was the brainchild of Michael Holroyd Smith, an engineer, who had been experimenting with electric traction since 1883. He had tested his ideas on a succession of narrow gauge railways, culminating in a third rail line in the Winter Gardens, Blackpool, where the town council was considering laying a tramway. After seeing both this line and a full-scale test track at Holroyd Smith's works in Manchester they took the daring decision to allow him to equip their proposed Promenade line with his electric conduit system. The Blackpool Electric Tramway Co Ltd was formed for the purpose, the first rail was laid on 13 March 1885, and the first tram ran under its own power in June of that year. Various faults in construction delayed the opening until 29 September, until which time a horse service was run, as it was whenever the electrical equipment broke down. The first year's operation was very successful, and considering the conditions facing the undertaking, the performance of the equipment, which suffered only two major breakdowns in 1887 and 1893–4, was very creditable. Problems included the relatively light and shallow construction of the conduit as compared with later examples, the mechanical and electrical breakdowns caused by sea water, sand and children's hoops getting into the conduit, and the difficulty of gaining access to make the necessary repairs. Later on boxes fitted with lids were provided on the original line to make it easier to attend to the copper conductor and its insulators, which gave continuous trouble, whilst Mapples' patent cast-iron conduit with hinged cover was installed on the last extension in 1897. Holroyd Smith's conduit had wooden sides to which the insulators were fixed with hardwood pins. No definitive record exists of the first 10 cars used on the line, and the story of the successful attempt to provide one, in *Blackpool by Tram* by Palmer & Turner, reads like a detective story. The cars were built by two firms, Lancaster and Starbuck, and the fleet was divided into winter and summer cars, all except two being double-deck with the usual open top. Nos 1 and 2 were built by Starbuck and were very advanced for their time in having transverse garden seats on the top deck. Nos 3–6 were all built by Lancaster with knifeboard seating on top, but nos 3 and 4 were smaller than the rest of the fleet and may have been used on the experimental line in Manchester. Cars 7 and 8, by Starbuck, had open sides on the lower deck and were of course meant for summer use, as were nos 9 and 10, which were single-deck open-sided trailers intended to be hauled by nos 3 and 4. Unfortunately the Corporation refused permission for the use of trailers, and so they remained

unused until they were eventually replaced by double-deckers in 1891—
for many years these latter cars were thought to have been the original 9
and 10 until further evidence came to light. The original fleet had no
separate trucks to carry the motor and axles, these being attached directly
to the car. The drive was taken to one of the axles, by a chain, whilst the
current collector was attached to the car by ropes in order that it should
break loose if it came up against any obstruction. Six further cars were
added to the fleet after the Corporation took over in 1892, and two new
extensions were made before all the conduit lines were converted to
overhead current collection in 1899.

Siemens and Halske had also been experimenting with conduit supply
during the 1880s, and its design for the Budapest tramways was the best
yet produced. In 1887 the firm built a metre gauge demonstration line in
the Hungarian capital from the West Railway Station for about a kilo-
metre along the Great Ring to Kiraly (now Majakovszkij) Street. The
success of this line led to the construction of the first permanent electric
tramway along Stacio, now Baross Street, two years later, and eventually about 16 miles of conduit route were constructed, although its high
cost meant that suburban lines were equipped with overhead from 1893
onwards. The S&H conduit was of the side-slot type with the conductors
in a channel under one of the running rails, and the system remained in
use until 1925. The original cars were built by the local firm of Ganz
with electrical equipment by S&H. They had a single motor driving
both axles via chains together with the normal open-balcony, clerestory-roofed body of the period. The saloon windows could be dropped
right down into the sides and the seats, including two on each platform,
were made of wood. The livery was red.

However by the time the Budapest line had been opened a much
simpler and cheaper alternative method of current collection had at last
been found. This involved the use of a trolley pole fitted with springs so
that it pressed a small wheel at the top of the pole up against a single
overhead wire. Van Deopole had begun experimenting with such a
system in the early 1880s, and in 1885 he built a mile-long line in
Toronto from a railway station to the site of an exhibition using a single
car equipped with a trolley pole. The motor car was capable of hauling
three trailers at 30mph, and the line, which proved a great success, was
not closed until the city system was extended to cover it in 1892. Van

Deopole did not immediately realise the significance of his discovery as he built a number of later lines using trollers. In 1886, however, he used trolley poles in Montgomery, Alhabama, and again in the following year for the first line in Massachusetts from the Thomson-Houston factory in Lynn. However other troubles continued to plague the lines of all the early pioneers—the motors were underpowered, the track was not strong enough, and no method of current collection worked for long. In fact in 1887, after all the efforts described above, there were only nine electric street tramway undertakings in Europe and 10 in the United States, with a total track mileage of under 60 and a fleet of about 100 cars.

The breakthrough came in 1888 as a result of the inventive genius and dogged persistence of another American, F. J. Sprague. He had been working on the problems of electric traction since the early years of the decade, and in 1887 he was awarded a contract to provide a complete electrical street railway system for Richmond, Virginia. At this time Sprague had little more than his already proven motors and a lot of ideas, which it was to take a great deal of trial and error to translate into practice. Problems were numberless—the track was badly built, the motors barely coped with the gradients, the wiring was constantly burning out, and it took forty attempts to hit upon the eventually successful trolley pole. But the line opened in February 1888, and despite continuing troubles more or less regular operation was attained by the end of the year, with 40 cars running over 12 miles of track, a greater mileage than all the other ten American systems open at that time. The operating company actually went bankrupt and Sprague lost a lot of money, but this was more than made up by the other contracts which were awarded to him on the basis of this initial success, the first and most important of these being for the electrification of the West End Street Railway in Boston. One of the problems which worried the management of the West End company was whether or not a line of cars starting together would overload the dynamos, and it was to prove the fallacy of this argument that Sprague arranged his famous simultaneous start demonstration in which 22 cars were lined up and driven off, without incident, one after the other.

Sprague's contribution to the development of the electric tramcar was immense, for although other inventors had found solutions to one or other of the problems involved, no-one had as yet succeeded in solving them all, or in putting all the answers together to produce a truly reliable electric tramcar. The equipment of Sprague's cars included trolley poles, series-parallel controllers, and motors mounted 'wheelbarrow fashion' supported partly by the axle, and partly by springs from the frame which reduced the effects of jolting over rough track. Worm gears replaced the more usual chains or belts. Van Deopole, of course, could claim a slight lead in the invention of the trolley pole, and this gave Thomson-Houston, who bought him out, the chance to become Sprague's main rival. Van Deopole was also responsible for another important improvement, namely the provision of carbon instead of brass brushes on the motors which decreased the wear caused by frequent starting. Another major innovation which was made soon afterwards was the fitting of the motors and gearing onto completely independent trucks, which freed the car bodies of the mechanical strains set up by the motors. But it was Sprague's Richmond line which proved to horse railway managements in the United States that electrification was feasible, so much so that within a year 200 streetcar systems, or trolley lines as they came to be called, were either working or being built, and almost all under Sprague's patents, whilst between 1890 and 1900 nearly the whole of the horse mileage was converted to electricity and the total street railway mileage tripled.

Progress in the rest of the world was far less rapid, although it did not take long for the first overhead trolley lines to appear. In Britain Messrs Waller and Manville, who had been involved with the Northfleet conduit line, built a trolley-equipped tramway to serve the Edinburgh Exhibition of 1890, although neither the counterweighted poles nor the sliding current collector were typical of modern American practice. The sprung trolley pole and wheel was introduced into England under the auspices of the Thomson-Houston Company, which installed their electrical equipment on some lines belonging to Leeds Corporation leading from the city centre to Roundhay Park. Span wire overhead was strung from steel poles, a power station and depot were erected, and six single-deck cars of the American pattern were provided to work the line, which was formally opened on 29 October 1891, with regular public service being provided from 11 November. The Roundhay tramway was only intended as a demonstration of Thomson-Houston equipment, and when Leeds Corporation decided to electrify the rest of its recently acquired system in 1896 the company withdrew its service, which was replaced by corporation cars about a year later, this being the first municipally-owned and operated electric tramway in the country. Other early British lines, which all used the standard open-top double-decker, included the Guernsey Railway, which was electrified by Siemens in 1892 using trolley poles mounted on one side of the car, a practice which was common on a number of early lines; the South Staffordshire Tramways line between Walsall and Darlaston, opened on 1 January 1893, also with side poles, but including a new innovation in the form of Dickinson's swivelling trolley which enabled curves to be followed more easily; and in 1895 the Kingswood—Old Market service of the Bristol Tramways Co, a system which was remarkable in that it retained its original style of open-top car right up until final closure during World War II. Progress thereafter was not rapid, largely because of the restrictions of the Tramways Act, but by 1898 there were 150 miles of electrified track and about 500 electric tramcars in the United Kingdom.

In other countries likewise the first trolley-equipped lines began to appear in the early nineties. In fact a Sprague line was already in operation between Florence and Fiesole in Italy in 1889, and France's first overhead wire tramway was opened at Marseille in 1893. The electric tram was spreading much further afield than this, however, for in the early years of the decade Japan's first line was opened by an American company in Kyoto, and the first electric tramway on the mainland of Asia was built in Bangkok. Not every line was an immediate success, of course. In Melbourne, where cable tramways were still being developed, the first electric line in Australia was installed between Box Hill and Doncaster in 1889, but its two small cars lasted no longer than 1896. But overall the trolley provided the technical breakthrough which the electric tramcar needed in order to expand worldwide.

Although single wire overhead became general from 1890 onwards, some undertakings used double wires and double trolleys resembling modern trolleybus equipment. The use of two wires, one positive and one negative, eliminated the normal return circuit through the rails which caused considerable problems when current leaked into the earth. Telephone circuits were affected, and a phenomena known as electrolysis corroded the metal pipes buried under the streets. The real cure was to bond the rails together electrically so that the current did not stray, but a number of over-cautious cities insisted on double wires. Such systems included Cincinnatti in the United States, Yokohama in Japan, and Copenhagen in Denmark where the double trolleys, which were used only in the city centre, lasted from 1901 to 1912. The London County Council also had to use double wires on its Woolwich—Eltham service in 1912 in order to avoid stray return currents interfering with instruments at Greenwich Observatory.

The success of the trolley, however, put Siemens in a difficult position, for it held no patents for its use. So the company pressed ahead with the design of its method of overhead current supply—the bow collector. A new extension of the Lichterfelde line was used for the first experiments in 1890, when a car was equipped with a large frame upon which two small square bows were mounted. In 1893 the whole line was converted for overhead collection, with the original cars remaining in use until 1896. Since the bow had proved so satisfactory, further, less cumbersome designs were produced. In 1891 experiments with a single, counter-weighted bow took place both in Budapest and in Frankfurt, where a line was laid along the Mainzer Landstrasse from the Hauptbahnhof to the grounds of the International Electrical Exhibition, at which, incidentally, a trolley equipped line was also shown by the Schuckert Company. The spring-loaded bow was introduced in 1893 in Genoa, Hanover and Dresden, and its use then spread fairly rapidly throughout western Europe. On the first lines the little square bows used in 1890 were reproduced, but in 1894 the more familiar triangular bow was introduced. Siemens also designed a large square bow for double-deck cars which was used in Hobart, Tasmania, this being very similar to the current collector fitted by Dr. Hopkinson to the Bessbrook cars in Ireland.

Once overhead current collection had been perfected it might have been thought that all the older methods would have been abandoned, but in point of fact both accumulator and conduit traction, together with a variant of the latter known as the closed conduit, continued to be used for some decades. The reasons for this were neither technical nor economic, for all the alternatives to overhead were either less efficient or more expensive, but what would now be called environmental. Many towns, particularly capital cities, objected to having overhead wires in their streets, and quite a number forbad their use, at least in the city centre. In Paris, for example, no overhead wires were permitted inside the line of the fortifications, and within those limits trams used all three of the available systems. Cars on the Villemomble—Place de la République route could operate on overhead, conduit or accumulator, whilst the important route Bastille—Charenton was electrified on the dual system of overhead in the outskirts and conduit in the city centre. The closed conduit system was introduced on 1 June 1896 on the route between Place de la République and Romainville. Also known as the surface contact system, this involved an underground feed wire which was tapped every yard or so by a metal stud which projected above the road surface in the centre of the tracks. When a car passed, and hopefully only when it passed, the stud was energised by powerful magnets and fed current to the motors via a skate underneath the tram. All these modes of operation were largely discontinued after some major floods in the city in 1910, which caused serious damage to the underground installations.

Other cities which used accumulator cars in their centres included Vienna, Berlin and Hanover. The Vienna line along the Ring was only a temporary expedient until a conduit was installed a couple of years later in 1900, and this lasted until wartime conditions forced its closure in 1915. In Berlin many routes crossed the central area where overhead wires were forbidden, and a fleet of no less than 321 bogie tramcars fitted for dual operation was built up. The accumulators were charged from the overhead supply, but sometimes not enough power was taken to cover the unwired section. Other Berlin lines were operated by conduit, especially after accumulators were forbidden in 1902. Two methods were employed, involving either permanently attached ploughs which could be raised and lowered at will or detachable ploughs which had to be fitted at each change point. Such frequent changeovers led to delays and breakdowns, and in 1907 overhead wires were erected throughout. In Hanover conduit was never used, and the city cars had accumulators fitted under the seats in the same way as in Berlin. In order to disperse the fumes nautical-style ventilators were fitted on the roofs of the cars. Hanover though had several long country routes, and it was not thought worthwhile to equip their cars with the heavy accumulators. So incoming cars picked up small trailers containing accumulators, an idea which might have been of benefit in other towns where batteries were used, for one of the main objections to them was the obnoxious fumes and the danger of acid-spillage. One of the few places to operate an entire system by accumulator was the historic Belgian town of Ghent, where in 1901 a total of six routes was in operation. Later on, overhead wires were introduced in the outskirts, and eventually over the whole system. There were quite a number of other continental cities, like Hagen, Milan, The Hague and Ostend which had one or more accumulator routes, but almost all had disappeared before World War I. The cars used in New York until the 1930s were exceptional, and were specially designed with lightweight, windowless bodies to take account of the fact that batteries could provide only a limited amount of power.

Accumulator traction was cheaper than overhead, but less efficient, whereas conduit was much more expensive, but worked at least as well, if not better in some circumstances. Later types of conduit as developed in the decade 1895–1905 were much stronger than Holroyd Smith's Blackpool installation, and were laid at a greater depth, being much more akin to contemporary cable installations. Construction in New York, for example, involved heavy iron yokes 5ft apart, with insultors bolted to every third yoke, which were accessible from the street. Rails and yokes were bolted together and the whole cemented in, the conduit itself being made of concrete. Two conductors were installed to provide a complete circuit, rail return being dispensed with. Cleaning manholes and drains were provided every 200ft, it being necessary to scrape the mud out monthly. Apart from the expense, problems included slot closure caused by expansion of the street paving, the need to make the slot, especially at the very complex junctions, substantial enough to take the weight of other traffic, the expense of relaying other underground services, and troubles with the plough. On the other hand, there was no problem with overhead repairs, no electrolysis where two conductors were used, and the system was cheaper to operate, or so early results in New York seemed to show; and, of course, there were no unsightly overhead wires. However, with one or two exceptions like Bournemouth, Brussels, Lille and Nice, it was only major cities like New York, Washington and London which could afford to pay the price to preserve their amenities. The London County Council's system, which was inaugerated on 15 May 1903, eventually totalled 123 miles, although outer lines were fitted with the more economical overhead, which meant that most cars had to be dual-equipped with ploughs and trolley poles. The changeover was effected at one of the 21 change points, where the plough was detached and run off into a little siding in the conduit where it was ready for the next incoming car.

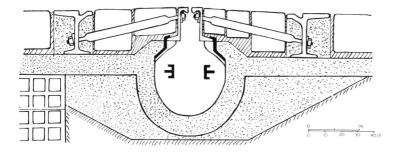

Cross-section of a conduit-fed electric tramway laid in New York in the late 1890s. The conduit itself is lined with concrete, and the metal members forming the slot are firmly bolted to the running rails. Cable construction was very similar

The surface contact system was never a serious contender, as although it was not as expensive as conduit, it was much less efficient. Apart from Paris, it seems to have aroused most interest in England, where the West Metropolitan was experimenting with the Lineff system as early as 1888. 200yd of track beside Chiswick depot were fitted with 3ft sections of central third rail under which, but not in contact, was a length of flexible hoop iron laid along the electrical conductor. When the car passed a powerful magnet lifted a section of rail to energise the motors, after which the rail dropped back into its original position. This system was never used commercially in England, but three others were—the Dolter, of French origin, in Hastings, Mexborough and Torquay; the Lorraine, derived from the United States, in Wolverhampton; and a home-grown product, the Griffiths-Bedall, in Lincoln. The least successful of these was the Dolter, although a fitful service was maintained at Torquay and Hastings between, respectively, 1907 and 1911 and 1905 and 1914. The line between Mexborough and Swinton in South Yorkshire, however, was an unmitigated disaster. It took nearly two years to build, longer than any other British street tramway, and once operation did start in 1907 complaints of live studs and dead horses multiplied! so much so that conversion to overhead began in March 1908, and the remaining Dolter services were compulsorily withdrawn in July. The Lincoln and Wolverhampton systems fared a little better, remaining open until 1919 and 1921 respectively. Experiments took place in a number of other places, such as Aberdeen, Leeds and London, where a prolonged effort was made to equip a line on the G-B system, but none of these came to anything. Indeed, even if the surface contact system had worked safely, which it did not, it would have been hard put to it to make any headway against the almost universal overhead wire, which by 1914 was used on almost all the tramways of the world.

CHAPTER FOUR

THE STANDARD ERA

BY THE YEAR 1900 the experimental stage in the development of the electric tramcar was coming to an end, and although many horse tramways remained to be converted, it was no longer a question of devising new techniques, but simply of applying those already known. From the turn of the century until the mid-twenties it was, as C. F. Klapper has aptly called it, 'The Golden Age of Tramways'; a period of about 25 years, coming a little earlier in the United States and a little later in Europe, in which the tram was the usual method of transport for the city dweller. Electric tramways were built in all continents and most countries, being absent only from central Africa and parts of Asia. Every town of any size in the Americas, particularly though not exclusively in the North, in Western Europe, the United Kingdom and Australasia was provided with a tramway system, all, or almost all, within the remarkably short space of only twenty years. The rapid replacement of horse by electric tramways was due to certain advantages possessed by the latter, notably the superior speed of the electric tramcar, which, at an average of 12mph, was about twice that of the horse car. This meant that vast new areas could be opened up for residential development, because people could live further away from their work, and yet the operator, with his larger and faster cars, could provide a better service with fewer vehicles, which meant that operating expenses were a smaller proportion of receipts than they had been with animal traction. The exhilerating possibilities of touching 20mph, moreover, encouraged people to ride who would not otherwise have done so—shoppers, holidaymakers and the like—which provided another boost to traffic figures. And of course with hindsight one can see that the electric tramcar enjoyed a great, though unrealised, advantage from coming to maturity during the infancy of the motor vehicle.

But as it was the development of electric tramways was dramatic and comprehensive. A few statistics will prove the point. In the United States on 1 January 1888 there were 172 electric tramcars running on 86 miles of track; eleven years later there were 41,402 cars and 14,782 miles of track, and by 1917 this latter figure had risen to 44,800. 5.8 billion passengers were carried in 1902, 11.3 billion in 1917 and the peak figure, 14 billion, in 1923. The industry was much smaller in the United Kingdom and its development was slower, but its impact on the towns was fully as great. In 1904 there were 6,783 trams in Great Britain, in 1910 there were 11,123, and throughout the twenties there were over 13,000, with a track mileage which had remained fairly static at around 2,500 since 1910. Particular examples reinforce the general impression of an electric tramway boom. In Sheffield, for example, the first electric tram ran on 5 September 1899 and the last horse car on 11 November 1902. Two years later the fleet numbered 237, by 1910 it was 264, and by 1920 it totalled 373. Further north, Glasgow had a system of 200 track miles with, by the mid-twenties, about 1,100 trams and 10,000 employees. Development was proceeding just as rapidly on the European continent where, to take one particularly well-planned example, Vienna had electrified its tramways between 1897 and 1903, with the single exception of a suburban steam tramway. By 1928 the system had grown as indicated in this table, and in that year over 651 million passengers were carried.

Year	Route (km)	Motors	Trailers
1904	184.28	955	880
1928	314.70	1703	2173

Most early electric tramcars were small, two-axle, single-deck vehicles, not much different from the horse cars they were replacing—indeed, they often *were* horse cars! The only exception to this rule was the United Kingdom, which continued, once the Roundhay experiment was over, with its double-deck tradition. However, despite their common origin, electric tramcars soon began to appear in all sorts of shapes and sizes, and quite distinct lines of development were followed in

Above The exposed position of the early motorman is exemplified by this Glasgow Standard car in original open-top half-canopied condition in 1903 [*Greater Glasgow PTE*

different parts of the world. At least three main streams of development can be distinguished—the American, the British and the European. Other parts of the world had their local peculiarities, but generally they tended to follow one or other of the major areas, usually because of a colonial or a trading link. The main point of interest in this period is the development of standard types of tramcar in each of these areas—hence the title of this chapter.

The first American streetcars—commonly known in the electric era as trolleys—were converted horse cars, but it soon became evident both that these were mechanically unsound and, with the new motive power, capable of considerable improvement. The horse car had been built as one unit with the wheels attached directly to the body, but once electric motors were fitted this set up unacceptable strains on the bodywork, which had, after all, been constructed to resist the pulling of a horse rather than the pushing of a motor. To counter these mechanical forces the motor was mounted in a completely separate truck, to which the body was attached via sets of springs, which also helped to iron out any jolting caused by poor trackwork. This solution was devised largely by J. A. Brill, of the famous firm of car builders of that name, and Brill trucks were to be found in many parts of the world for years afterwards. For example they were used under the Glasgow Standard cars, and two types of early motors built for Munich in the 1890s were known as the 'short' and the 'long' Brill classes for the same reason. So far as American car bodies were concerned, horse car designs were carried on almost unchanged, except that it was now possible to build them both larger and stronger. The typical American car in the 1890s had a body up to 20ft long mounted on a two-axle truck. The driving platform might be open, as on a horse car, with gates to close off the sides. Some of these early electric cars had a passage way in the front dash to facilitate train operation, which was quite common at the time in North America, actual horse cars often being used as electric trailers. Toronto provides an example of both these operational techniques, and the last horse car was not withdrawn until the early twenties. The practice of screening the platforms, either by a windscreen or by a totally enclosed vestibule with doors, took hold much earlier in America than elsewhere, probably because of the very severe winters. So far as the passenger accommodation was concerned, both open and closed bodies were provided, just as in horse car days.

As street railway traffic grew cars larger than the standard two-axle vehicle became necessary. Four-wheel trams cannot be lengthened beyond a certain limit, for the truck has to be short enough to negotiate curves—the maximum wheelbase of a two-axle truck being about 9ft— and if the body is carried too far over the ends of the truck the car begins to plunge like a ship at sea, with disastrous results for the track. The solution was the eight-wheel bogie car, which had already been employed on both steam and cable tramways, and which was first introduced on an electric tramway in either Boston or St Louis. Normally a bogie with four equal wheels needs a motor for each set of wheels to obtain sufficient adhesion, a practice which is followed on most modern cars today. But at the time this was felt to be too expensive, and Brill designed a bogie known as the maximum-traction truck with one set of large powered wheels and another of small 'pony' or guide wheels. The advantage was that eighty per cent of the weight was distributed on the driving wheels, which overcame the adhesion problem. As a matter of fact Anthony Reckenzaun had designed and used such a truck in his battery experiments in London in the 1890s, but Brill's was the first commercial application of the principle, which made bogie cars almost as economical to operate as the standard four-wheeler.

Thus the second generation of American trolleys built around the turn of the century were long eight-wheelers having a much higher capacity than their predecessors. The public, however, continued to demand open cars in the summer and closed cars in the winter, a fact which gave street railway managements considerable headaches. To begin with two fleets were provided, one for the summer and one for the winter, but this proved an intolerable expense. The next step was to provide two sets of bodies which could be changed at the appropriate seasons, which at least cut out the cost of providing duplicate trucks and electrical equipment. The ideal, however, was a single car which was suitable for year-round use. One contender was the California type of combination car already developed for use on cable tramways, and quite a number were built on the same pattern as the cars still running in San Francisco with a closed section either in the middle or at one end. The trouble with these, though, was that people did not have a personal preference for one section or the other, rain or shine, but all crowded into the saloon when it was raining, and vice-versa. Another expedient, which was used in Toronto from 1904, was a car which could be converted from closed to open simply by removing the side panels and rearranging the seats, but this still did not meet the difficulty of unseasonable weather. The car which came nearest to satisfying all the conflicting demands made upon it by management and public was the convertible, which could be altered from closed to open simply by raising the side panels into the roof. Two designs were current. One, known as the Duplex, had curved body members enabling the curved side panels to be slid up into the roof where they overlapped, leaving the sides completely open. The other, built by Brill, had straight sides with hinged panels, which again, windows and all, could be pushed up into the monitor roof. Such cars had a considerable vogue in the early years of the century, but they were not ideally suited to city traffic, where longitudinal seats were preferred to the cross benches necessary on open cars, and they were naturally more expensive to build than ordinary cars.

A feature of American tramways, which was much less common elsewhere, was the considerable pleasure traffic which was both demanded of and encouraged by the street railway companies. Obviously holiday resorts such as Atlantic City might expect such traffic, but in most cities and towns a trolley ride to the park became, for a time, one of the most popular ways of spending a summer's evening. And if there was not a convenient park available, the company would often build one—naturally at the end of the line—and provide such facilities as amusement parks and dance halls to attract the customers. In 1902, for example, Massachusetts street railways owned 31 pleasure parks between them and one of them, the Holyoke Street Railway, derived over $1\frac{1}{4}$ million of its $6\frac{1}{4}$ million passengers from this source. This meant that Sunday and holiday traffic was relatively heavy, sometimes almost touching the weekday average, which was naturally beneficial in that the fleet was kept active over the whole week. It also meant that the heaviest traffic load occured in the summer months, which was one reason why open or convertible cars were so necessary. By 1930 this had all changed—people were finding their entertainment elsewhere, holiday traffic was now only about half that of a weekday, and peak traffic now came in January rather than June, all of which helps to explain the virtual disappearance of the open car.

Another disadvantage of open cars, from the company's point of view, was that fare evasion and pilfering by conductors was all too easy, with passengers getting on and off anywhere along the car's length. The innovation of the system known as Pay-as-you-enter (PAYE) in Montreal in 1905, and its rapid adoption elsewhere in North America, signalled the end of both the open and the convertible car, and also, by making all passengers pass the conductor's desk, cut down both pilfering and fare evasion. What with the demise of the open car and the increased odds against dishonesty, the companies seemed to be having it all their own way! But there was one problem with PAYE—namely the increased loading time inevitable when passengers had to wait before passing into the main body of the car. The solution to this was the provision of a large platform so that passengers could all board at once and allow the car to move off. Several designs were produced, the most common probably being that with a platform at the rear. This meant that cars had to become single-ended, as opposed to normal tramway practice, so turning wyes or loops had to be provided at terminii. Another wellknown design was the Peter Witt, named after a Cleveland street railway commissioner, in which passengers boarded at the front and then paid their fare to a conductor stationed at the centre of the car, after which they either left by the centre doors or went to sit down in the rear. The Toronto Transit Commission put a fleet of 575 of these cars into service in 1921–3 as replacements for some of the out-dated company stock, much of which had wooden bodies, no doors to the platforms, and only a stove for heating. The new cars had steel bodies, air-operated doors, adequate heating and modern electrical and safety features. All-metal construction, incidentally, was developed very early in America, well before World War I, when most European trams were still built entirely of wood. Oddly enough the only remaining large fleet of Peter Witt cars is to be found in Milan, where the backbone of the fleet is still made up of 501 such cars dating from 1928–30, and which are only now being rebuilt for one-man service. Another popular design of trolley was known as the nearside, in which the conductor was stationed just behind the large front door through which passengers both boarded and alighted, except on some later models in which a central exit was added. Particularly popular in Philadelphia, where 1,500 were put into service between 1911 and 1913, the nearside was so-called because it was designed to serve stops on the nearside of crossroads, as opposed to farside stops where rear-entrance cars were thought to be better.

Thus it was that the American standard car of the 1920s was a long bogie vehicle of all-metal construction, with straight sides, as opposed to the inward curving sides characteristic of older cars, and often with such refinements as air-conditioning, folding doors and air brakes. The top speed was about 30mph, and current collection was almost universally by trolley pole, except on the conduit equipped systems mentioned in the previous chapter. Out of the tens of thousands of such cars the only ones remaining in public service on the North American continent—except for a tourist service in Toronto—are 35 operated on the St Charles line in New Orleans. These particular cars were built by the

Perley Thomas Car Co, are 46ft 8in long, 8ft 4in wide, 11ft 4in high, and seat 52 people. They were reconditioned for further service in 1964 and were recently converted to one-man operation, but apart from this are typical of the American standard in its heyday.

There were, of course, considerable variations within the standard, and also exceptions to it, some quite widespread. Trailers were fairly common in the United States, much more so than in Britain, but on the other hand double-deckers were few and far between. Such vehicles seem to have been most popular with lines catering for holiday traffic where the extra capacity was welcome and where the slow loading of the double-decker, which seems to have been the main American objection to them, was less objectionable. Contrary to early British practice the top deck was usually covered with an awning or a more permanent cover, often with side curtains to unfurl in case of rain, just like the Adelaide horse cars mentioned in an earlier chapter. Some city systems did experiment with double-deckers, including New York where an enormous centre-entrance car worked unsucessfully for a while, and Pittsburgh, where, by a strange coincidence, the first double-deck car built by the Pittsburgh Railway Co carried the same number, 6000, as the New York car.

It was not only the crowds which worried street railway men about the time of World War I, but also the rapid escalation of labour and material costs, coupled with the first breath of motor competition exemplified by the famous, or infamous, Jitneys—early motor cars which began to ply for hire and, assisted by their novelty value, managed to make a hole in company traffic figures for a few years. One way of coping with this problem was to produce larger and yet larger cars, the most far-reaching development here being the articulated cars produced in Boston by linking two old trolleys with a central section, of which more later. Less successful were the attempts to splice together old cars into long rigid vehicles, examples of this being provided by Toronto and St Louis. Another possibility was to use small, one-man cars, and to meet this need the Birney Safety Car was introduced in 1916, to prove an immediate success. These little two-axle cars—a few bogie versions were also produced—had a specially light construction to economise on materials and current, which, when coupled with their economy on staff, proved an irresistible attraction to managements, who bought thousands of them before the boom broke as suddenly as it had begun in 1921, when it became clear that these small cars were no solution to the problems either of peak hour traffic or of growing motor competition.

The British standard car was quite different from the American, and was a product not of replacement of earlier designs, but of a gradual process of evolution in which certain features remained constant right up until the end of the period. The majority of British trams were single truck, the only major exception in the nineteenth century being the Middlesbrough fleet designed by J. Clifton Robinson, although of course the larger cities soon found the higher capacity of the bogie car an attraction. In its earliest form the standard type of tram had open platforms and an open top, which might or might not be extended over the driver's stance. Where canopies were fitted they were less for the comfort of the motorman than for the increased capacity afforded on the top deck, as in the case of the Glasgow horse cars which were provided with canopies when they were electrified around the turn of the century—electrified horse cars were, incidentally, quite rare. Seating consisted of longitudinal benches in the lower saloon and either knifeboard or garden seats on the top deck, although the latter soon became the rule. Typical of this period were the cars used in Bristol, which were all two-axle, uncanopied open-toppers, with three or four saloon windows, a design which remained unaltered until the last car was built in 1920, and indeed until the last tram ran in 1941. In fact, with the exception of some single-deckers, none of the systems in South-West England ever owned a tram with a roof!

Elsewhere, however, various improvements began to be effected from the turn of the century onwards, the most notable of these being the introduction of top covers. The British public seems to have been as firmly wedded to the open air as its American cousins, for most early top covers were designed to admit copious draughts of fresh air, or even to be totally removeable when conditions warrented it. Some early experiments involved the use of canvas screens, as in Leeds where two cars were fitted with enclosed ends linked by a trolley plank from which were suspended striped canvas awnings, and in Liverpool, where early versions of the cover designed by the manager, C. T. Bellamy, used canvas for the roof and sides. The latter was a most distinctive design with an arched roof whose panels could either be slid up into the centre or unbolted and removed, and with windows which could be wound down into the sides, leaving the top-deck completely open apart from the arched metal struts used to support the roof. Very similar covers were marketed by a firm called Milnes, Voss under the name of the Magrini cover, and it is likely that these too were based on the Liverpool manager's work. A variant idea was the Kennington cover, one of which was supplied to Hull, and which worked on the principle of the roll-top desk. Sometimes, of course, top covers were left open for economy's sake rather than with any idea of passenger comfort. The London United Company, for example, fitted 102 cars with ends and roofs in 1910–11, but left the sides as they were, with wrought-iron railings. Later on sides were fitted, but even then the windows were left unglazed, with sprung blinds to pull down in case of rain. However, it soon became evident that convertible covers were unnecessary in the British climate, and more permanent designs soon began to be produced.

The most widespread development after this time was the fitting of permanent roofs extending the full length of the car, the first of these being designed and fitted by A. D. Day, tramways engineer of Bolton Corporation, in 1903. In this case only a fairly small area, about a third of

Below   This Liverpool scene shows a line of Bellamy-roofed cars about 1910 in a street
devoid of all else except horse-drawn vehicles   [*H. Hewitt-Cooke*

Above A line of trams in King Edward Street, Hull, about 1910 with their Kennington covers open [*Collection J. S. Nicholson*]

the whole, was enclosed in the centre of the upper deck, the remainder forming two open balconies at either end. Cars of this type continued to be built well into the interwar period, and indeed they provided perhaps the best balance yet between covered and open accommodation.

One or other of two further improvements was then made to the standard tramcar body. Some undertakings, such as Burnley Corporation or the Kidderminster and Stourport Company, provided screens for the driver's platform, whilst others fitted overall top covers. The first of these was introduced in 1903 by the Great Grimsby Street Tramways, and the rights to this design were taken up by Milnes, Voss which sold some to places like Birkenhead. The LCC was one of the first large undertakings to make fully-enclosed top decks standard, although curiously enough police regulations made it impossible for it to enclose

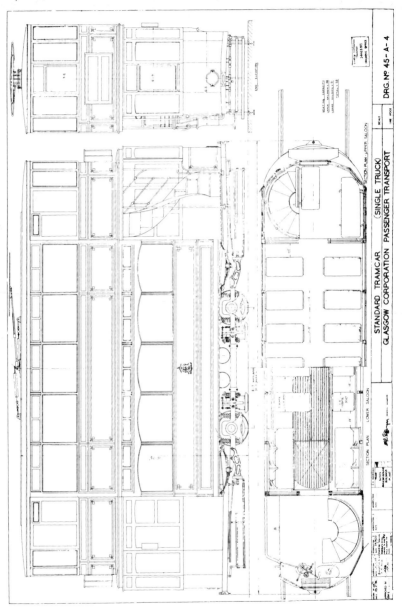

A Glasgow Standard car as modified with 8ft wheelbase truck and fully-enclosed upper
deck after 1928   [*Greater Glasgow PTE*

the driver's vestibules until well after World War I. But when both these improvements were combined, the result was a totally enclosed car; so far as the body was concerned, almost the final stage in the development of the British standard tramcar, apart from later more streamlined examples, like the Sheffield Roberts cars built after World War II.

A perfect example of the gradual evolution of the British tram is afforded by the Glasgow Standards, the first of which were built as open-toppers from 1898 onwards. The next phase involved the fitting of top covers to the existing cars and the building of a series of new trams to this specification which took place between 1904 and 1910. In phase three all cars were vestibuled and provided with roll-top storm covers over the stair heads, by which time there were over a thousand Standards in the fleet, which in the final phase, from 1927, were given fully-enclosed bodies and, for the most part, longer trucks and higher speed motors. It would be impossible to allude to all the many varieties of the standard car, often distinctive to the city they served, for many of the larger cities, like Glasgow, built their own cars, and even those which did not insisted on their own local specifications to a degree unknown today. There were the Birmingham cars, uncommonly narrow because of their 3ft 6in gauge; Sheffield's light and airy Standards, some surviving right to the end in 1960; London's trams, most notably the LCC E1 class, of which there were a thousand; Brighton's fleet of home-built open-toppers, and the assorted cars of the Manchester conurbation. There were many more, yet all were distinctively and unquestionably British—double-deck, angular, and rather old-fashioned, but with an inexhaustible capacity for moving people.

In most cases British trams were the products of two or even three firms—the makers of the truck, which was often American-built, the suppliers of the electrical equipment, and the body builder. These included firms like Brush, Hurst Nelson and Milnes as well as the larger municipalities, such as Glasgow and Liverpool. It was the builder which usually assembled the complete tram, unless it was more convenient to do so at its destination, rather in the same way as the modern motor car is assembled at the manufacturer's plant. The method of construction remained very conservative right to the end of the period under review, with the car body generally being made of wood, on an underframe either of oak with steel reinforcement or of rolled steel sections. The inward curving 'rocker panels' on the sides were retained until quite late in many designs, such as the earlier Sheffield Standards. The floors were of pine boards, with slats of hard wood for wearing purposes, and with two or more removeable traps fitted over the motors as inspection hatches. If the car was a four-wheeler, the truck might be one of a variety of types which had been developed to overcome various problems. The simplest had rigid axles, but this tended to give a poor ride, to overcome

Below   A class D maximum-traction bogie car with an overall top-cover on the London County Council's conduit system. The three lights above the destination indicator were for a short-lived route-colour system

Above Sheffield Standard car 206, built in the Corporation's Queens Road Works between the wars, photographed at Woodseats terminus in 1959

which the swing or pendulum axle truck was developed. These were fitted with special springing which took up irregularities in the track, a well-known example being the Brill 21E, as used under the Glasgow Standards. A major disadvantage of the two-axle truck was its inability to negotiate short-radius curves, to overcome which the radial truck was devised. This permitted radial movement of the axles, either by allowing the axle boxes to move within the side frame, or by pivoting two sub-trucks onto the main car frame, the only major user of the latter being Leeds Corporation. The best solution, of course, was the bogie truck which, as already mentioned, might be either maximum traction or equal wheel. The wheels themselves were either made out of cast iron with a chilled rim—a relic of horse car days—or increasingly of steel with a separate and replaceable tyre. Mechanical equipment included a selection of the four available types of brake, always including a hand brake, and one or more of the mechanical track brake, the magnetic track brake or the air brake, sometimes supplemented by rheostatic braking from the controller. The electrical equipment was relatively simple, consisting of two or four motors controlled by resistances and fed from an overhead wire via a trolley pole.

British permanent way was particularly solidly built, because local authorities demanded high standards, and indeed the very first British Standards related to tramway track, which almost universally consisted of heavier versions of the grooved girder rail developed towards the end of the horse tramway era. British rails had narrower and shallower grooves than their American counterparts, which reflects one of the objections to Train's trams in 1860. Apart from this, American, British and European track was very similar, but in other areas, such as Russia and Japan, the use of Vignole rail, on the precedent set by Moscow tramways, was continued. The extremely robust nature of the best electric tramway track is illustrated by that laid on the LUT's Kingston extensions. Rail at 100lb yd was used, each section being joined by H-section anchors as well as being bonded electrically with copper wires. Sleepers were laid every 9in bedded in concrete foundations, which were paved with wood blocks. In other cases granite sets might be used. Items such as points and crossings were usually supplied by a specialist builder, in this case Edgar Allen & Co of Sheffield. Later on, the track joints on this system were thermit welded to reduce noise, a practice which later became almost universal on tramways. The overhead consisted of hard-drawn copper wire, at this period usually round, but later on more normally with a groove along the top so that it could be clipped onto the supporting ears and span wires. The LUT overhead was supported on centre poles in Southall and Ealing, and in other places side poles were used, but on the London system as elsewhere span wires, supported either from adjacent buildings or from side standards, were the general rule.

There were naturally exceptions to the British standard tram, and in fact single-deckers were rather more common than one might realise, either as a direct imitation of continental or American prototypes or for operational reasons. In the first category come the Hamburg-style motor

and trailer sets used for Liverpool's first electrification in 1898, as well as
the 12 American centre-entrance cars later used in the same city. And
north of the border Glasgow's high-speed car 1089 was a direct imitation
of American practice. In other cases, such as Gateshead and Cardiff, low
bridges forced the use of single-deck cars rather than double-deckers on
certain routes when, in order to obtain comparable capacity, extremely
long bogie vehicles were used. A few undertakings, such as Barrow and
Middlesbrough, used California cars, but these were not common. The
LCC owned a large fleet of F and G class single-deckers to work the
Kingsway Subway, which was only built to take single-deck trams, but
these were rebuilt into double-deckers when the subway was reconstructed in 1930–31.

In other cases it was low traffic rather than low bridges which dictated
the use of single-deckers, when small two-axle units, such as the three in
the Carlisle fleet, were more appropriate. When the troubles which had
affected America began to hit Britain, operators' thoughts naturally
began to turn towards one-man operation. Designed earlier than the
Birney was the Raworth regenerative demi-car, similarly a small, lightweight car designed to be operated by one man, with the added feature
that when the motors were used as brakes they actually fed current into
the system, a selling point guaranteed to appeal to the manager of any
small, struggling system. It was in fact only to such systems that these cars
did appeal, and only a few were ever built for such diverse places as Glos-
sop, Barrow and the Yorkshire Woollen District. In a few other cases
existing single-deck cars were converted into one-man vehicles, one of
the most comprehensive experiments being made by the LUT, which
rebuilt four cars into its type S1, with such features as ticket machines,
pneumatic doors and fail-safe braking systems, but these were withdrawn in 1928. In most cases British, in common with continental tramways retained the traditional two-man crew.

Other non-standard cars were to be found in the special conditions
obtaining in holiday resorts, where much of the fleet was only needed in
the summer. The absolute minimum of accommodation was afforded by
the toastrack car, which was just a mobile platform with seats on, boarded, like American open cars, from a footboard along the side. Many seaside resorts, like Llandudno, Southport and Blackpool, had a fleet of
these. Lytham had some double-deckers with open-sided cross benches

below and garden seats on top, the design being very similar to two of
Blackpool's original conduit cars. In other cases the open top and the

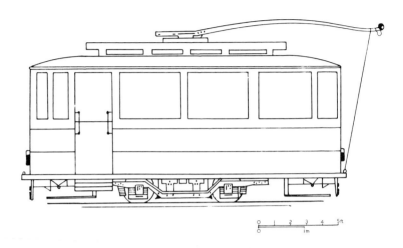

Example of the small one-man Demi-cars used on a few British systems until about 1920.
The contrast between these and the standard double-deckers could hardly be more
marked   [P. N. C. Cooke

open balcony tended to last rather longer than elsewhere. The Llandudno line, for example, used open-toppers right up until its closure in
the 1950s.

In the early days of electric traction quite a number of British systems
hoped to use trailer cars, probably initially as a way of using up service-
able horse cars. Bristol in fact did run horse car trailers for a short while. In
other cases trailers were specially built to match the new motor cars,
something which happened, for example, in both Hull and Leeds. Leeds
used its on the first corporation electric line between Kirkstall and
Roundhay, whilst Hull ordered a total of 25 double-deck trailers from
the same builder as Leeds, Milnes of Birkenhead. In neither case did operation last beyond 1901, and none of the early experiments ever became
more than that, probably because, with the low-powered motors of the
period, trailer operation was found to be too slow, quite apart from the
fact that the Board of Trade was loth to grant permission for trailers on

safety grounds. It did permit it in one or two cases during World War I, as for instance in Barrow where two trailers were used to deal with the heavy munitions traffic. The only large-scale example of trailer operation in this period was on the LCC system in London, where, after initial experiments with eight old horse cars, 150 new open-top trailers were built for use on four southern routes, where they remained in service between 1913 and 1924, providing a useful saving in manpower during the war.

In complete contrast to Britain, the use of trailers was the rule rather than the exception on the European continent, where the standard tram was a small, two-axle single-decker, very little different from the type used in the first decade of electrification in America. To obtain adequate capacity, it was necessary to operate these trams in trains, and strings of them winding through the streets were a hallmark of European cities for upwards of 50 years. As in other areas, old horse cars were sometimes rebuilt to provide the first electric services, and they were frequently used as trailers. In Brussels, for example, where the first electric line between the North and South Stations was opened in 1894, 26 horse cars were motorised and others used as trailers. In addition a large open car, seating 50, was specially built, the whole installation being carried out by the Thomson-Houston Co. Hanover provides another example of the use of converted horse cars, in this case electrified by Siemens in 1893 and using their early design of bow collector. Frankfurt-am-Main began electrifying its tramways in 1899, but here the horse cars were only used as trailers, a total of 61 open and 98 closed cars being reused in this way. The first purpose-built electric trailers were not purchased until 1905. Street scenes of this time provide an interesting contrast between the new electric cars and their erstwhile horse-hauled trailers, the main difference being one of size. Otherwise the design was much the same, at least as far as closed cars were concerned—electrified open cars were not at all common.

Once electric tramcars began to be built for the job, a more-or-less universal type began to appear. This was a two-axle, open-balcony, clerestory-roofed car, normally operated in trains of two or three. It seems strange that the Europeans did not follow the American example of providing vestibules much earlier than they did, and one can only imagine that it just did not occur to them that open platforms were no longer

Above   Munro Park, Toronto, in 1900 with a train of open-cars headed by motor 505,
built by the Toronto Railway Co in 1897   [*Toronto Transit Commission*

necessary now that the horse's reins had been dispensed with. Whatever
the reason, though, the open-balcony remained a typical feature for 10
or 15 years, after which screens began to be added to existing cars and
fitted as standard to new ones. After that the European standard car
changed surprisingly little, at least in appearance, for though new trucks,
new motors and lengthened platforms might be added in successive
rebuildings, the archaic clerestory-roofed outline was retained. And
even when that was dispensed with in the thirties, there was still no general departure from the well-tried two-axle design, which remained
dominant in most European countries until well after World War II.

   An excellent example of the evolution of the European standard tram
is provided by Copenhagen, where a fleet of over 900 single-truck cle-
clerestory-roofed cars was built up between 1901 and 1930. Most of the

system at this period was under the control of one company, A/S De Kjobenhavnske Sporveje (DKS), whose standard type of motor tram was a wooden, open-platform saloon, usually with trucks and equipment by UEG or S&H and with bodies by Danish firms. Between 1909 and 1910 all motor cars received screens to protect the motorman and the passengers from the weather, and in the following year the first fully-enclosed cars were delivered. These and all subsequent standard cars were built by the Danish firm of Scandia. In 1911 the DKS was taken over by the municipal Kobenhavns Sporveje, who put into service three further series of rather larger fully-enclosed cars. The trailers were a more haphazard collection, consisting of some old horse cars, 150 built new under the auspices of the DKS, half of which were open-sided cross-bench trailers, and a later standard KS design which initially had open platforms. Production of motor cars ceased in 1918 and of trailers in 1920, after which all the older vehicles were modernised in the KS workshops. This involved fully-enclosing the platforms, fitting new

Below Worn-out track being replaced at the junction of Queen and Yonge Streets, Toronto, in 1921. The wooden monitor-roof cars represent the second generation of American streetcars [*Toronto Transit Commission*

motors and controllers, some new trucks, upholstered seats, electric heaters, a new sanding system etc in the first stage, and in the second, between 1935 and 1938, fitting track brakes together with some new and
more powerful motors. Some of these cars completed over 50 years of
passenger service before the postwar run-down of the tramways caused
their withdrawal.

Copenhagen, with one major exception to be mentioned later, had a
particularly standardised fleet. In other cases there was more difference
between earlier and later electric cars, and a longer period of experimentation before a standard design was produced. Hanover, for
example, began with 18 electrified horse cars which were fitted with
motors, trucks etc, and then rather curiously followed these with 14
newly built cars without separate trucks. These little cars had a capacity
of only 16 seated and 13 standing. Some slightly larger cars were built in
the next few years, together with a series of 100 trailers delivered in
1898–9. Up to 1911 no large deliveries of cars were made, but instead 10
motor cars of varying designs were put into service between 1905 and
1912, from which was derived a standard series of 59 motors and 122
trailers, all of which had two-axles, four-window saloons, and a square
clerestory roof cut off at the bulkheads. To begin with doors were not

Below The last steel-bodied standard cars in service in North America are those on the
St Charles line in New Orleans [*New Orleans Public Service Inc*

Above The Australian drop-centre design is represented by Melbourne's class W7,
dating from 1955–6 [*Melbourne & Metropolitan Tramways Board*

fitted, the platforms being protected by gates. At the same time older cars
were provided with glazed screens. Between 1925 and 1928 a second
major series of standard cars was acquired, all except two with the standard four-window saloons, but with rather longer fully-enclosed platforms and a lengthened clerestory swept down over the ends of the car.
The motor cars had a capacity of 24 seated and 33 standing, almost twice
that of the 1893 cars. These were the last cars to have wooden bodies and
clerestory roofs, as from 1928 steel bodies and domed roofs began to be
introduced. The 1925–28 series were the first to be fitted with rheostatic
brakes, which replaced the older type of compressed air brake used since
the turn of the century. The air pressure for these was derived from a
mechanical compressor linked to the axles, which meant that the cars had

Above Copenhagen 205, built in 1903 for the DKS Co, and photographed at Østrigsgade in 1963, wears its fifty years rather well

to travel for about 500m before enough pressure was available to work the brakes. From 1927 all the older cars were fitted with electric brakes, apart from those used on line 11 which had the more normal arrangement of motor-driven compressors. As in the case of Copenhagen, these standard cars remained in service until well after World War II, the last being withdrawn about 1960.

This type of tramcar was more-or-less universal throughout Europe. In Gothenburg, for example, electric services were opened in 1902 with open balcony motors of type M1, which were quite quickly replaced by vestibuled cars of a similar size. Larger cars were introduced from 1921, and older ones were rebuilt to the same standard, which involved

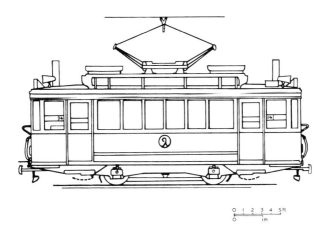

Two-axle clerestory-roofed trams were used almost everywhere on the European continent. This particular example is from Basle, Switzerland [*P. N. C. Cooke*

stronger trucks, improved electrical equipment, and the substitution of pantographs for bow collectors. Pantographs were introduced on a number of European tramways at around this time, and since then they have gradually replaced both trolley poles and bow collectors almost everywhere, although they were rarely found in either America or Britain, where one of the few towns to use them was Sunderland. The main advantages of pantograph collection are that the number of overhead supports can be reduced and maintainance costs are less as compared with tramways using trolley poles.

Just as in other areas, there were of course exceptions to the European standard trams, even in the period under review. Both Berlin and Munich, for example, built up large fleets of maximum traction bogie cars almost from the first, and these remained the standard type of tramcar in Munich throughout the first half of the century. Two-axle trams were used in 1895 for the first electric route between Färbergraben and Isartalbahnhof, but in 1898 the first of the bogie cars, the type A, was

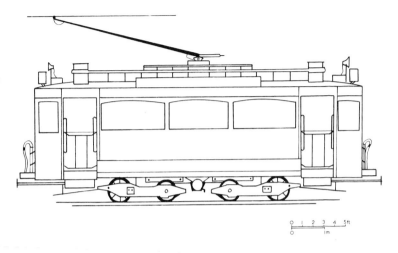

The first of the long series of maximum-traction bogie cars used in Munich was the A type, introduced in 1898   [*P. N. C. Cooke*

delivered, the last series, apart from some post-war rebuilds, coming with the type F in 1929. Just like the contemporary cars in other cities, these went through various stages of rebuilding. The type D, for example, consisted of a series of 100 motors and trailers built by the Munich undertaking itself between 1910 and 1913. They were first rebuilt in 1926–31, and again in the 1950s, involving such changes as the replacement of the trolley poles by pantographs and the trellis platform gates by doors. These cars had conventional front and rear platforms, but in other cities such as Lyons and Kattowice centre-entrance bogies were to be found. In quite a number of cases a small series of bogie cars would be acquired to work a particular route or service in a town which otherwise remained wedded to the standard two-axle unit. Gothenburg's route to Långedrag, which was regarded as a light railway, was a case in point, and was supplied with three totally enclosed cars as early as 1908, although these were not bogies, but were fitted with radial axles. However in 1922 the undertaking took delivery of its first six bogie cars for this line, the extremely handsome type M21. And the Kattowice centre-entrance cars mentioned above were intended for a new express tramway service introduced in 1931 between Gleiwitz and Beuthen (the city, now in Poland, was then a part of Germany). Other cities experimented with bogies, but later went back to single-truck cars, Vienna—where a small series of type T maximum traction bogies was built in 1900—being a case in point.

The other way of increasing a tramcar's capacity—by adding a top deck—proved even less popular on the continent than the use of bogies. Just about the only example of a complete system being operated by double-deckers is afforded by the A/S Frederiksberg Sporveje, the smaller of the two companies operating in Copenhagen at the beginning of the century.

As a generalisation, then, one can say that the standard American tram was a fully-enclosed, single-deck bogie car; the British standard car was a double-decker, either bogie or single-truck; and the European standard tram was a two-axle single-decker, operated in trains. Generally speaking the rest of the world tended to follow one or other of these patterns, often because of a political or an economic relationship. Thus the South American countries have always used cars of an American pattern, more often than not secondhand from the United States, and it was quite possible until recently to see cross-bench open cars, Birneys and enclosed standards hard at work in these countries long after they had disappeared in the north. In the same way certain British colonial territories, such as South Africa and Hong Kong, used typical British double-deckers, and in fact Hong Kong is one of the last two places in the world to do so. Similarly North African cities like Algeria and Tunis tended to follow French practice. In other cases a rather more indigenous product has emerged. Australasia, at the time a part of the British Empire, seemed to draw inspiration from both Britain and the United States, for though some systems, such as Hobart and Wellington, used double-deckers for a while, the most common design of tram came to be the bogie single-decker. The typical Australasian variant of this, though, was the drop-centre car with entrances in the middle, a good example being the Melbourne Class W developed in the 1920s as a replacement for the cable trams. In the Far East, Japan was very much influenced by American practice, and the typical Japanese tram was a bogie single-decker of rather austere appearance. Other parts of the Far East evolved their own designs to suit local conditions. Indian trams, for example, have usually been large bogie vehicles suited to moving large crowds, whereas those in Singapore and Bangkok seem to have been designed to suit the climate, with a large proportion of open and unglazed cars in their fleets. A most interesting tramway system was built up in Shanghai, which was not a colony, but parts of which had been taken over by certain foreign powers as trading posts. A separate tramway system was built up in both the French and the British Settlements, with through running taking place from 1912. The British section was opened in 1908 by the Shanghai Electric Construction Co Ltd. By 1936 the fleet amounted to 107 motors and the same number of trailers running over 35 track miles. The nightly maintainance schedule includes an interesting item—washing throughout and disinfecting! The trams were continually being rebuilt and modernised, and indeed the system is still running under Chinese control. The company, incidentally, printed tickets both for itself and for the Hong Kong and the Singapore tramways.

Tramway systems do not only differ in respect to their trams, but have expressed their individuality in all sorts of other ways. For instance during the period under review it became general practice to distinguish routes either by numbers or by letters, these being displayed on the tram together with the destination. Various means have been adopted to do this, including stencils, wooden boards, metal plates, and the by-now almost universal roller blinds. Some systems, though, persisted with the use of colour codes, particularly on the continent, where quite a number of systems still uses them, especially in Belgium. One of the most complete examples was provided by Copenhagen's tramways, which had coloured route number plates by day and pairs of coloured lights by night—route 5, for instance, had black numerals on an orange ground with, after dark, two orange lights. British examples included the LUT, which painted its cars in at least four entirely different liveries for separate groups of lines, and Glasgow, where the standard cars had a coloured band painted around their top deck, a system which lasted there until World War II. In other cases colour light codes were used, as in Edinburgh and on the LCC during the early 1900s.

The function of tramway depots is to provide covered accommodation at night together with facilities for day-to-day maintainance, and they are therefore pretty standard structures throughout the world. British tramways generally liked to have all their cars under cover, but on the continent, where there were large numbers of trailers to cater for, outside storage sidings beside the depot were more common. Some undertakings liked to have their buildings tastefully designed, and quite a number of tram depots could qualify for the local equivalent of Scottish baronial architecture—for example, Köpenick depot in East Berlin could well be described as 'Strassenbahn baroque'! American companies seem to have been less prone to such corporate extravagance, and their sheds were often of wood, which was all very well except in case of fire, which is an ever-present risk. Indeed quite a number of small American tramways lost their fleets in this way.

A group of cars often forgotten is the works cars, of which every tramway had a certain number, often converted from old passenger vehicles. There were basically four types—water cars, snow clearance cars, those connected with track and overhead maintainance, and a fleet of general purpose trailers. Water cars were used in early days to dampen down the dusty road surfaces of the time, and later on, when this function was no longer necessary, were sometimes retained to ease friction on sharp curves. Instead of this Leeds had permanent track fountains on some of its corners to assist the passage of the over-long trucks of the Pivotal cars, whilst Bradford had taps on some steep hills to keep them useable in greasy conditions. The American style of water car had a big cylindrical tank on the back and long pipes which could be swung out to sprinkle a wide area of the road, European examples being found in Hull and Frankfurt, amongst other places. British tramways usually covered the tank in with a box-like body.

A variety of cars were used for snow-clearance, including salt cars, snowploughs and snowbrooms, the latter being most common in areas with severe winters, like North America and Russia. Track maintainance involved open cars suited to carrying materials like sand, sets and rails, an example being a series of 12 cars used in Gothenburg which looked rather like steeple-cab locomotives, only with an open 'truck' section fore and aft. Overhead maintainance required tower wagons and wire trucks from which new wire could be reeled off, though in this case a fleet of road vehicles was also necessary so that repairs could be carried on without obstructing the service and independently of the power supply. Other types of works car included cable-laying vehicles, tool vans, stores vans and rail grinders.

Another specialised fleet was built up on some tramway systems for the carriage of goods. Huddersfield, for example, had a service of coal trams from a railway yard to various mills, and there was a similar service in Leeds up to the 1920s. In other cases railway wagons were worked over tramway metals, which required either that the tramway was laid with sleeper track—as on the Blackpool and Fleetwood Tramroad, where a steeple-cab locomotive was used to haul coal wagons to Thornton Gate sidings—or, if grooved rail was used, that its gauge was 4ft 7¾in, which was the case in Glasgow where some shipyard traffic was worked over tram lines in Govan. Quite a number of tramways ran parcels services, examples being provided by Carlisle, where trade was especially good in eggs and luggage, and Falkirk, where the company's advertisements exhorted, 'When ordering goods by Telephone, tell your Merchant to forward by Car'. Postboxes were also provided on tramcars in some towns, including Huddersfield, Birmingham and Amsterdam. Perhaps the most bizarre type of traffic was the funeral cortege, to cater for which quite a number of tramways built special cars, including Durban, which had two funeral trams, and Gothenburg, where there was a fleet of five hearse trailers between 1918 and 1936. Milan even had a special tram line to serve a large cemetery, with purpose-built rolling stock running from a funeral station in the city centre.

The variety of uses to which trams have been put is too great to mention here. They have been illuminated and decorated to celebrate or advertise particular events, such as coronations or wartime recruitment drives; they have been used as ambulances in wartime, as in Hanover in World War I, and as first-aid posts in peacetime, as in Dresden; one turned up as polling station in Invercargill, New Zealand, and another as a soup kitchen in Halifax; yet another as a library in Munich, and two more as a 'Sandman Express' for mothers and toddlers in Dresden, whilst Santa Claus rides annually on a tram in Zurich and a cable car in San Francisco. Interesting though all these variations on a theme are, however, the vast majority of trams has always been perfectly ordinary—the standard tram performing its standard task of getting people to and from their work and leisure, a function which many tramway operators in the 1920s seemed to think was theirs by divine right. Their complacency was soon to be rudely shattered.

CHAPTER FIVE

BEYOND THE CITY BOUNDARY

THE TRAM in Britain has been regarded as a largely urban creature, only venturing into the green fields on the occasional dash between city and suburbs. As far as the rest of the world is concerned, however, this has certainly not been true in the past, and even now there is a considerable mileage of tramway running between rather than within centres of population. In considering such lines a careful distinction must be drawn between North American and European practice, for this has been almost entirely different on almost every count. The American interurbans were, as their name implies, intended primarily as links between cities and smaller towns on their periphery. The typical European line, which may be called a rural or country tramway, tended to serve much smaller places, and was usually regarded less as a link between large centres of population than as a service to the rural community. The American interurban would serve such places if they were on a fairly straight line between A and B, but the European country tram would wander hither and thither so that the tiniest place could be served. The differences between the two types of tramway are also partly due to the fact that they had an entirely different history. The interurban was a product of the electric era, and in fact most of them lived and died within 40 years. Country tramways, on the other hand, very often began life in the nineteenth century as rural light railways operated by steam, and frequently went through a stage of petrol or diesel operation before final electrification, which in many cases did not happen at all. The first of them were laid 10 or 15 years before the interurban boom, and quite a few are still running today.

Because of their different history and their different purpose, the interurban and the country tramway evolved quite different modes of operation. Interurbans may best be described as heavy tramways, normally built to standard gauge and employing many of the features of steam railroads, including viaducts, bridges, signalling, terminal stations, and segregated tracks. The cars were usually much larger and heavier than their city counterparts. The European lines, on the contrary, tended to be built to a lighter standard than city tramways. They were often of a narrower gauge, whilst their track was usually very lightly and economically built, often being a single track running alongside the road. The cars were not greatly different from the standard two-axle vehicles used in the towns. Such lines had much of the charm of narrow gauge light railways, whereas the interurbans, at least in their heyday, were much grander affairs altogether.

Having drawn the distinction it must immediately be qualified, for some European lines are much more like interurbans than the country tramways which have been described. Examples of past or present European interurbans include the Köln-Bonner Eisenbahn between Cologne and Bonn, the two trunk routes out of Düsseldorf to Duisburg and Krefeld, and Hanover's famous line to Hildesheim. Such lines have a considerable proportion of segregated track, often employ signalling, are normally double track, and have tended to use cars much larger and heavier than those on the town systems, though this is less obvious now with the great increase in the size of urban trams.

One further problem is that it is often extremely difficult to make a logical distinction between interurban or country lines and those which are simply prolongations of urban tramways, or which have a purely suburban function. Each case has to be decided on its merits. For example up until 1956 there were two routes between Lille and Roubaix in northern France. One was operated by the town tramways, whilst the other, which is still open, by the clearly interurban Société Nouvelle de L'Electrique-Lille-Roubaix-Tourcoing. In other cases the character of a line has changed over time, usually due to urban sprawl. Thus the Philadelphia Red Arrow lines were originally interurban, but they would now better be described as suburban. The same is true of some of the surviving Belgian light railways, particularly those in and around Brussels and Charleroi.

The first true interurban in North America opened in 1893 between Portland and Oregon City, but in common with other early lines it was not very successful, and was actually bankrupt within a year. The new electric cars were simply not yet reliable enough for long distance, high speed operation, and did not become so until the early years of the twentieth century. From 1901 to 1908, however, there was a tremendous boom in interurban building, interupted only by a financial crisis in 1904–5. The peak mileage of 15,580 in the United States was reached in 1916, though this official figure ignored many lines in New England which were prolongations of street railways linking independent communities—if such lines are included the total might well rise to something more like 18,000 miles. The interurbans were not spread evenly over the country, but were concentrated in states like Ohio, with nearly 3,000 miles, Indiana, Pennsylvania and Illinois, with around 1,500 each, and in California, with over 1,000 miles. They were least thick on the ground in the South and in the mountain states. Canada had about 850 miles of interurban, over half in Ontario, where they were known as radials. This incredible expansion was partly due to effective promotion, and to the growing feeling that a place was not anywhere unless it was on an interurban, but largely to the very evident advantages possessed by this new system of transport. It proved to be a very effective means of transporting people over distances of anything up to 200 miles, whilst a considerable freight traffic was also developed. Part of this expansion was achieved by opening up new areas, which provided an opportunity for the very profitable practice of buying up large areas of undeveloped land, running an interurban through them, and then waiting for the profits to roll in—a scheme brought to perfection by Henry E. Huntingdon, the millionaire proprietor of the Pacific Electric Railway in California. The interurbans also expanded at the expense of the steam railroads, who in some cases, particularly in New England, attempted to buy the interurbans out, and in others put obstacles in their way when they needed to cross the railroad tracks, making costly embankments, bridges and underpasses necessary.

None of this, however, was able to stop the progress of the interurbans, which by the time of World War I had built up vast networks in various parts of the country. Almost half the total mileage was concentrated in the Middle Western states, where it would have been quite possible to travel from Milwaukee to Detroit, Cleveland to Indianapolis, and Cincinnatti to Detroit, together with a myriad of other permutations. It was theoretically possible to travel the 1,087 miles between Elkhart Lake, Wisconsin, and Oneata, New York State, in the years from 1910 to 1922, and tickets were actually issued for the 267-mile journey from New York to Boston which involved fourteen changes of car and one overnight stop. A magnificent dream, which came to nothing, or almost nothing, was the Chicago-New York Air Line, which was intended to connect the two cities by a 750-mile double track laid to permit regular speeds of 90mph. The route would have cut 200 miles off the steam railroad journey, but the impossibly expensive standards of construction coupled with an inopportune depression meant that only 30 miles of main line were ever built, and this had to be ignominiously linked to Gary, La Porte and Chicago by ordinary track to form a local interurban. The only other memento of the great dream was two superior Niles cars, lettered 'Chicago' on one end, 'New York' on the other.

More normal interurban journeys would have been from Terre Haute to Indianapolis, or Milwaukee to Chicago. Indianapolis was the centre for about a dozen lines, and in 1904 a vast new terminal was built to serve them. By 1912 cars were coming and going at a rate of 500 a day, and 7 million passengers a year were passing through it. Trains with observation cars, dining cars and sleeping cars ran over the Mid-Western lines, often at speeds of up to 60 or 70mph. The Mid-Western network was made up of a large number of independent lines, but in other areas consolidations resulted in some extremely large individual companies. A number of minor lines around Boston, for example, combined in 1899 as the Eastern Massachusetts Railway, and further amalgamations produced the Bay State Street Railway, which extended from Rhode Island to New Hampshire. It had 950 miles of route, over 2,100 motors, 30 trailers, 158 service and baggage cars, and numerous snowploughs and other works cars. These New England lines were not true interurbans, the principal characteristics of which were high speeds and a large proportion of private-right-of-way (prw). A comparison with other states with interurbans makes this clear. In 1907 Massachusetts had 2,886 miles of street railway, of which only 9.2 per cent was prw, whereas Indiana had 67 per cent of its 1,932 miles on prw. And in 1902 maximum interurban speeds in Ohio, Indiana and Illinois varied from 40 to 60mph, whilst the highest speed in Massachusetts was 35mph, and only one other line out of 75 had cars capable of a maximum of 30mph.

The most famous of these large systems was the Pacific Electric Railway, which began with a line from Los Angeles to Pasadena in 1893, and was built up by Henry Huntingdon to a route mileage of over 700, with four-track main lines, five-car trains, and colour light signalling. Main Street passenger terminal in Los Angeles had seven tracks, and there were also two sheds in the freight depot which handled both parcel and full carload traffic. Huntingdon had his own private car, the *Alhabama*, which was fitted with bedrooms, kitchen and dining room, and whose four 200hp motors could produce a top speed of over 90mph. After World War I the *Alhabama* was sold to the Sacramento Northern, which used it for private hire work until, in 1931, a fire in the kitchen destroyed the car. The 'big red cars' of the Pacific Electric connected such exotic places as Los Angeles and Long Beach, Hollywood and Beverley Hills, and their tracks formed greater Los Angeles as it is today. But the system was over-extended, and the first local routes closed as early as 1924, and the last route in 1961. Amongst the effects of this was the isolation of the negro community of Watts, which, as a major junction, had been created by the Pacific Electric, and was now left to find a new identity in the midst of the most automobile-conscious city in America.

The standard interurban car in the early years was a wooden-bodied bogie vehicle with a monitor roof swept down over the ends, and powered by four 140hp motors which gave a top speed of about 60mph. From 1910 steel bodied cars began to be introduced, and these domed-roof vehicles became more typical during the inter-war period. Later speeds were much higher too, with average speeds of up to 70mph, even touching 80 on the straight. Races with parallel steam lines were quite common, and one interurban even had a publicity film shot showing a car overhauling an aeroplane. Until the very last years interurban cars were much larger than their city counterparts, sitting very high on their bogies, and with a cowcatcher at the front. Like the railroads, they had to give warning of their approach by a bell or a whistle, the former being used on the street-running sections at the beginning or end of a route. Current collection was usually by trolley pole and overhead wire, though other methods were experimented with, like pantographs or third rail collection. Interurbans were very prone to accidents, due to such deficiencies as excessive speed, ineffective brakes, long lengths of inadequately signalled single track and, at night, poor lighting. A head-on collision, with an aggregate impact of over 100mph, could be disasterous—33 people were killed in such an incident in Indiana in 1910.

Not all interurban companies were large ones like the Pacific Electric, and small ones like the Niagera, St Catherines and Toronto Railway in Canada were probably more typical. This line, which incidentally never ran to Toronto, opened its first route between St Catherines and Niagera in 1900, and various extensions brought the route mileage up to 30 by 1908. The maximum mileage was achieved between 1926 and 1929, when there were five separate routes radiating from St Catherines, but in the latter year the passenger service to Niagera Falls was withdrawn. After various cut-backs the final passenger service was withdrawn in 1959 and freight services were dieselised in 1961.

In point of fact most interurbans had succumbed to the combined onslaught of the automobile, the truck and the motorbus well before World War II. The Bay State network was in the receiver's hands as early as 1917, most of the New England lines had closed by the end of the 1920s, and virtually the whole interurban network collapsed during the great depression after 1929. Only a few lines survived in the 1930s in Iowa, Illinois and California. Many companies fought back with improved services and the new lightweight cars, and at least one line tried to beat the bus at its own game by adopting an invention known as the Evans Autorailer. This vehicle, which was based on a Ford bus, had both rail and road wheels, and in the mid-thirties it displaced the heavy electric cars on the Arlington and Fairfax interurban. It ran on the track to a convenient level crossing and then on rubber tyres to a community not served by the interurban, in which way it could go right into the centre of Washington. Of course it soon became obvious that buses would be much simpler, a conclusion which was reached nearly everywhere on the continent. No classical interurban line now exists in North America, and the years of their dominance were surprisingly short, often no more than thirty years.

European rural and interurban tramways, on the other hand, have had a much longer life, some of them dating from the age of steam, others from the electric era, and many surviving well into the motor age. In a very few cases such lines began as horse tramways, a mode of operation which seems to have been particularly common in the flat terrain of the Netherlands, where an interurban was opened between Den Haag and Delft as early as 1866—a line which is, incidentally, still in use as part of the urban electric tramway system. The longest of these equine inter-urbans was that between Zuidbrook, Stadskanaal and Ter Apel, a journey which involved several changes of horses. Generally, however, horses were not thought suitable for such long trips, and the widespread development of extra-urban tramways had to await the design of an effective steam tramway locomotive, which was achieved in the mid-1870s. In discussing these lines one is faced with the problem of defining the difference between a tramway and a light railway. Most countries have drawn a legal distinction between the two, but this usually refers to such things as safety precautions, methods of financing etc, rather than to any operational differences, so it is not a great deal of help in distinguishing a train running in the street from a tram running across country. Hard and fast distinctions cannot really be made, and as usual there is an uncertain area between the two transport modes. A distinction sometimes, and probably without any official backing, made in Switzerland is based on the provision of toilet facilities! Trams don't have toilets, trains usually do. However a working definition of a tramway might be that it runs for at least part of its length in or alongside the road, and that it uses tramway type vehicles. The typical rural steam tramway ran in the street only in towns and villages, most of its length being made up of roadside track, with the occasional cross-country diversion.

Motive power became standardised in the form of the fully-enclosed four or six-coupled tramway locomotive, whilst the passenger stock normally consisted of two-axle carriages, though larger bogie versions were sometimes used. Many lines provided wayside stations, often quite elaborate affairs with ticket offices, waiting rooms and station houses, and sometimes even including such refinements as weighing machines! These latter could be found on Brussels-Wavre tramway in Belgium. Most rural tramways were built with the intention of carrying both passengers and goods, so a varied fleet of goods wagons and vans would be built up, and sidings were provided at stations, factories, and even in the fields where farm produce could be loaded directly into the wagons.

The first steam-operated lines in both Holland and Italy were opened

Above An 0–6–0 steam locomotive heads a long train on the Belgian Vicinal at Edingen near Brussels [*SNCV*

in 1879, respectively between Den Haag and Scheveningen and between Milan, Gorgonzola, of cheese fame, and Vaprio d'Adda. Two other famous cheese towns in Holland, Edam and Gouda, were also later brought into the steam tramway network, a situation which might have prompted some enterprising travel agent to offer a cheese tour of Europe by tram! France seems to have been ahead of both these countries in the development of steam tramways, there being 411km in operation as early as 1880, rising to 1,085km by 1890 and to 9,715km by 1912. Other countries never approached this mileage, which, when coupled with the 12,000km of light railways, was excessively high, and many of the lines never paid their way. Nevertheless roadside steam tramways were important in many other areas, for example around the northern Italian industrial cities, such as Turin, Milan and Brescia. The latter was the centre of quite a network of lines going as far as Mantua, 44 miles away, of which Baedeker's Guide for 1903 pointed out that 'numerous wayside stations are stopped at, and punctuality is by no means assured'! Probably the most famous Italian steam tramway was that between Milan and Magenta, opened in 1879–80, and operated by steam right up until its closure in 1957. Most of its locomotives were of the enclosed tramway type, built by the Austrian firm of Krauss, apart from some secondhand vehicles acquired later. Milan was also the centre for Italy's largest network, the Tranvie Inter-Provinciale, which incorporated the original Adda line, and which at one time owned as many as 80 enclosed tram locomotives. Another Milanese line between Monza and Bergamo, which did not close its final section until 1958, was operated by a mixed bag of fully enclosed and partially enclosed steam locomotives, supplemented in later years by battery tramcars, which cost more to run, but which had the virtue of cleanliness! Country tramways were not subject to the same restrictions as those in towns, and often used the cheapest, and dirtiest, forms of fuel.

The most concentrated network of steam tramways in Europe was to be found in the Low Countries, where the pioneer line to Scheveningen was followed by about 30 others before 1885, all of them, surprisingly in view of later events, in Holland. These included the lines between Haarlem and Leyden, Flushing and Middelburg, and quite a number around Amsterdam. The Rotterdamsche Tramweg-Maatschappij (RTM) laid its first rural tramway in 1898 to the rather uncommon Dutch gauge of 1.067m (3ft 6in), and between then and 1915 built up a network serving the five islands south of Rotterdam. Many of the routes were separated by waterways, and special ferries were built to carry goods wagons between the islands. Most of the steam locomotives were of the railway type with only the motion enclosed. Nearly all of the Dutch steam tramways, which were to be found in almost all of the 11 provinces, had been closed or electrified by the time of World War II, but some of them, like the Gelderse Tram, were resurrected to provide passenger transport during the occupation. Holland was also the home of Machinefabrik Breda, which built a total of 306 steam tramway locomotives for the home and overseas markets. The Netherlands possessions provide almost the only example of the use of European-style steam tramways in colonial territories. As late as 1941 there were 10 steam tramway companies still active in Indonesia, and it was recently discovered and reported in *Modern Tramway* No 396 that some of these lines were still running under the auspices of the Indonesian Railways. For example the former Oost Java Stoomtram still operates between Udjung, Surabaja, Wonokrono and Karang Pilang, the inner part on city streets, and the outer forming a typical Dutch roadside tramway. A large part of the fleet of o—4—o tram engines was built by Beyer Peacock, although the Dutch firm of Werk-spoor is also represented; only one or two of them are still needed for the twice-daily passenger service to Karang Pilang and the limited amount of urban and freight traffic.

The rural tramway, either steam or electric, has now completely disappeared from Holland itself, though it still survives in neighbouring Belgium. As we have seen, that country was left behind in the construction of light railways, and in 1885 the Belgian government set up a national body, the Societe National des Chemins de Fer Vicinaux (SNCV), to construct such lines 'with the express object of enabling agriculturalists to compete with foreign producers' (Cole, *Light Railways*). This momentous decision eventually resulted in Belgium having the largest single tramway system in the world, a system which was of untold importance to the economy of the countryside, not least in two

Below   An SNCV diesel *tracteur* hauls a goods train through the woods near Poix in the Ardennes [*SNCV*

world wars. The SNCV had a monopoly on the construction of all light railways, and also provided the rolling stock, the capital for this being derived largely from national and local government. Operation, however, was entrusted to private companies, who hired the line and equipment from the Society. In this way a truly national system was developed, with common rolling stock and, in most cases, a common gauge of one metre, although a proportion of the lines were constructed to the Dutch gauge and others to standard gauge. This meant that lines could be linked, and rolling stock interchanged, wherever desirable—something which the haphazard development in, for example, France, made impossible. Some of the early lines to be built included those between Antwerp and Turnhout in 1885, Ostend and Blankenberghe in 1886, Sprimont and Polseur in 1887, and Brussels and Humbeek in 1889. The first of these was built on the 1.067m gauge with the possibility of connections with the Dutch lines in mind, whilst the Sprimont line, of standard gauge, was one of the last to use steam engines. The haulage of stone from a local quarry finally ceased in 1966. The line from Ostend, and part of that between Brussels and Humbeek, are still in use as electric tramways. By 1895 there were 1,307km of light railway, 2,600km by 1905, 3,802km by 1915, with a peak of 4,812km reached in 1940. Over this whole period the unelectrified mileage constituted well over half the total, although, as will be seen, it was not all steam operated.

The Belgian light railways occasioned such interest that various reports on them were commissioned by the British government, one of which was submitted to the Board of Trade by a Major Addison of the Royal Engineers in 1894. At that time the SNCV was working 58 lines with a total length of about 730 miles, whilst four more lines, 40 miles in length, were being built, over 80 per cent of which were metre gauge. Slightly over a quarter of receipts came from goods traffic, for which sidings were provided at main line stations and for private companies and individuals. The society had 245 locomotives, most of them weighing 18 tons, but some as much as 30 tons. There were 663 passenger carriages and 1,574 wagons and luggage vans.

Major Addison travelled on the 12½ mile Andenne-Eghezée line, a roadside tramway, in a mixed train, which accounted for the fact that the journey time was normally 1hr 25min, though one train each way was timetabled at only just over the hour. On lines like that between Ostende and Furnes, which were chiefly intended for passengers, speeds were a little higher, in this case 1¾hr for 20 miles. Regulations in fact prescribed maximum speeds of 30km/h (18mph) in the country and 10km/h (6mph) in the towns. The locomotives in use on the Andenne line were typical Vicinal fully-enclosed, double-ended 0–6–0s. This design had been adopted in contrast to many other European steam tramway undertakings which stuck to the 0–4–0 wheel arrangement, largely because of the sharp radius curves on many such lines. The Milan—Magenta fleet, for example, was almost entirely two-axle. However the SNCV considered that 0–6–0 engines were particularly suited to roadside tramway operation where speeds were not high, and over the years they continued to produce a succession of designs. Around 1895 most of them, like the one the Major inspected, weighed about 18 tons, but later designs were larger and heavier. For instance, one of the most common classes was the Type 18 which weighed 22 tons in working order, and had a tractive effort of 2,945kg. Standard gauge locomotives, of course, weighed even more—for example, no 813 of Type 12, which was built in 1906 for the Groenendaal—Overijse line, weighed 28.5 tons in working order, and exerted a tractive effort of 3,537kg. Most of the engines were built by Belgian firms, such as the Societe St Leonard of Liege and the Société Métallurgique of Brussels, though a quirk of history meant that some of them were constructed by English builders such as Hawthorn of Newcastle. During World War I the Vicinal routes behind the allied lines had great strategic importance, and 50 engines were built for the use of the British Army; 48 of these, together with some coaching stock, were bought by the Vicinal after the war.

One wonders whether Major Addison's report was taken down and dusted in 1914 though the peaceful scene he describes could not have been of much interest to the War Office. His train was made up of a passenger carriage, having both first and second class accommodation, a luggage van, and one goods wagon. Carriages were normally two-axle, though a few bogie ones were built, and first and second class, composite and brake coaches were provided. The luggage vans were built to the same dimensions, and incidentally carried a post office letter box for the convenience of those living on the route. Various improvements were made to the coaching stock over the years—open platforms began to be screened from 1913 onwards; the wheelbase was gradually lengthened from 1.80m in 1886 to as much as 2.80m in the last composite cars built for steam service; teak was replaced by metal bodywork in World War I. Goods wagons were of various types, though the majority were 10 ton open trucks. The major's train dropped its goods wagon en route and picked up three others, which had already been loaded in the sidings provided alongside the main line. The train stopped at fixed points, where there might be an inn used as a waiting room, or just a notice board. There were no signals on this particular route, and they were only used in exceptional cases, usually to cover level crossings or swing bridges. In 1890, for instance, there were ten signals on the line between Ostende and Furnes.

World War I and its economic aftermath caused radical changes in the SNCV. Many of the operating companies became bankrupt, and the society was forced to become an operator, a process which was virtually completed when the coastal route was taken over in 1956, leaving only one small tourist line, the Grottes de Han, in private hands. Steam operation became increasingly uneconomic, and as well as closing or electrifying such lines, the SNCV embarked on an almost unique policy of using petrol or diesel-powered trams instead of steam engines. It is true that there were examples of this in Holland on, for instance, the Gelderse tramway and on the RTM which began using railcars from 1925, and from 1947 built up a fleet of these and of diesel locomotives which took over all remaining services from 1956. But the SNCV operation was unique both in the vehicles used, which were a cross between a railcar and a locomotive whilst remaining unmistakably a tram, and also in its scale—300 of these *autorails* were built to run throughout the Belgian countryside. After various experiments the first standard petrol tramcar was produced in 1933. It had a wooden body, double-ended, with the same square outline typical of any urban electric tram of the period. The motor was mounted centrally with the exhaust pipe leading up through the roof, and the car had a two-axle truck. A few bogie vehicles were later produced, metal replaced wood for the bodywork from 1935, and diesel engines were fitted instead of petrol. Most, if not all, were fitted with seats for passengers, but they were capable of hauling considerable trains of wagons or carriages, some of which were specially built for these autorail services. The SNCV itself no longer operates any autorails, as all its non-electrified services have been abandonned, although one or two are retained for works duties, including ART 300, the last to be built. This was turned out in 1949, the body, interestingly enough, by the works at Andenne, and with its extremely powerful 165hp engine was used to haul heavy trains. A few autorails still haul passengers on the privately-operated Grottes de Han line, where traffic is so heavy that AR 266 had to be taken out of a museum to work the line!

Generally speaking, of course, steam tramways were succeeded by electric lines, as was the case with a considerable mileage of the SNCV. In Germany steam tramways seem to have been much less common, although there were some like the Oberrheinische Eisenbahn Gesellschaft (OEG), which opened in 1887 and did not withdraw its last steam tram until 1954. More usually rural tramways in Germany seem to have been electric from the start, like the extensive country system round Hanover. The first section dated from 1894–5, and by 1901 the six lines were complete, one of them running over 25km to the neighbouring town of Hildesheim. The system was in fact developed too rapidly, as the returns did not justify the high investment, and the tramway director of the time, Herr Krüger, was asked to resign. The lines were intended for both passenger and goods traffic, and as early as 1897 experiments were made in hauling ordinary farm wagons on sets of detachable flanged wheels known as *Rollböcke*, although a regular goods service was not introduced until two years later. Experiments continued with this idea of road-rail vehicles, and some goods wagons were equipped with sets of wheels for both road and rail, but this house-to-house service was brought to an end in 1911. Three rather similar vehicles, known as Bonner wagons, were used around the turn of the century on the Manx Electric Railway, one of Britain's few genuine interurbans. Goods traffic, however, proved to be the salvation of the Hanover country tramways, and for a time before World War I they formed the largest goods tramway in Germany, with, for example, traffic totalling 400,000 tons in 1911. All kinds of goods were carried, such as coal, potash, cement, milk and sugar beet. Hundreds of goods wagons were needed for this traffic, even including special trailers owned by the local breweries. At first ordinary passenger trams were used to haul the goods trains, but later special cars with stronger motors and van-type bodies were used—for example no 801 was built in 1928 for the carriage of milk. In addition the undertaking rebuilt six motor cars into electric locomotives. About 30 special tracks were provided for the goods traffic, including sidings into sugar factories and a brewery, a line to the canal basin at Misburg, and two long lines at Bilm and Ilten. These two latter lines were goods only, except that on Sundays and festivals special cars ran to take people to church. Goods stations were also provided in the centre of Hanover and at some other points, together with numerous dispatching and loading points. Goods services, whose receipts had at one time exceeded those from passengers, were eventually withdrawn in 1953 as a result of motor lorry competition.

The Hanover lines were built to standard gauge, and most of them consisted of the normal single-and-loop roadside track, the only exception being route 11. This route was also exceptional in using bogie cars, all the others being operated by two-axle motors and trailers. The motors used on these lines in later years came from the first series of metal-bodied cars produced for the city in 1928–30. They had a very distinctive external appearance, with no clerestory, square destination indicators mounted on the roof at each end, and a deep metal sun-vizor over the windscreen. Amongst the mechanical improvements incorporated were underfloor controllers and rail brakes. Most of these routes were very long, the exception being route 21 from Rethen to Pattensen, which was only a branch off route 11. That to Mehrum and Sehnde, for example, was 36km, and route 10 to Gehrden and Barsinghausen was 28km. By the 1950s, however, the decision had been taken to close the country lines. The outer section of route 15, between Sehnde and Mehrum, had in fact already been cut off before the war, although the track still led forlornly on from Sehnde depot until the route was finally closed. The remaining routes were closed in stages from 1951 to 1961, leaving only the inner section of route 11. In 1958 there was only this, together with route 21 and the inner parts of routes 10 and 15. All of these started at that time from a double loop at Am Klagesmarkt in the centre of Hanover, and probably the most attractive of the remaining lines was that to Gehrden, a small town to the south-west of the city. Cars ran along urban tracks as far as Badenstadt, after which the track singled to run along the lefthand side of the road on its own reservation. At a road junction called Sieben Trappen one of the old sidings was still to be seen, at which point the track bore left for Gehrden, a pretty little timbered

German town, where the cars terminated on a loop outside the depot. Trams still carried the destination 'Barsinghausen', but passengers had to change to buses in Gehrden. The depot faced right onto the street, which was so cramped that the track fan had to be at the rear of the pleasant tiled buildings, which in 1958 were already shared with the bus fleet, an arrangement which came to an end in 1961 when this, the last truly rural route, finally closed.

In many other countries former steam tramways were converted to electric operation around the turn of the century. For example, the still existing interurban routes around Vicenza in Italy are the result of such a conversion, as were the former lines of the Chemin de Fer Economique du Nord around Valenciennes in northern France. These extended for about 40 miles (64km) over the mining countryside on the usual roadside track, the most distinctive feature of the system being the two looped embankments and overbridges at railway crossings, and the rolling stock, which apart from the elderly two-axle enclosed motors and trailers, also included a series of open-balcony trailers. In Holland a number of routes were brought together to form the North-South Holland Transport Company (NZH). Amongst those existing in 1901 were the standard gauge steam line between the Hague, Voorburg, Leyden and Haarlem, another steam route, this time metre gauge, from Amsterdam to Pumerend, and an electric line, also metre gauge, from Haarlem to the seaside resort of Zandvoort. All these lines, together with others, were later combined into the NZH, which was interesting both for its variety of gauges and of cars. The Amsterdam–Zandvoort line, for example, was operated by 30 bogie cars built by Métallurgiques of Belgium in 1904, and later taken over from the original operating company, the Electrische Spoorweg Maatschappij. Some of this company's trailers were later converted into somewhat severe looking motors, whilst some control trailers which ran on this line were built by Ganz of Budapest. The most famous trams to be operated by the NZH were a series of articulated cars built for the standard gauge service between Haarlem, Leyden and the Hague. Their claim to fame is that they were the first such cars in Europe to be purpose-built, as opposed to being made up from older vehicles, although strangely enough they were not adopted in many other places until well after World War II. By that time the NZH itself, like so many interurban tramways, was in decline, and in

1957 the Zandvoort line closed, leaving only a group of lines around Leyden, which have themselves now disappeared. The 'blue trams', as they were known, seem to have inspired great affection amongst the people they served—it is still possible to buy postcards of the tram in Voorschoten, one of the little towns through which it passed.

The SNCV, in Belgium, has been a little more fortunate in that some of its lines still remain. The first electric route was opened as early as 1894, when the former steam tramway from Brussels to Petite Espinette was reopened. Other electric lines were gradually opened, so that by 1915 there were 413km of them. The peak of 1,511km was reached in 1952, but as late as 1971 there were still 279km in operation. The routes which remain are largely suburban commuter lines around Brussels and Charleroi, together with the superb interurban along the Belgian coast. The electric trams never reached into quite the same rural fastnesses as the steam and diesel trams did, but even so many of their routes went miles into the country. For instance it was once possible to travel by tram from Quievrain on the French frontier—which was itself on a tram route from Valenciennes—via Mons and Charleroi to Namur, and it is still possible to travel almost the entire length of the Belgian coast by express tram. The early electric rolling stock looked much the same as the contemporary steam trailers, with two-axle trucks, open platforms, and provision for two classes. The first cars had only handbrakes, but from about 1900 compressed air brakes were fitted, the roof-top cylinders for these having to be recharged at certain places with the necessary equipment. A very varied fleet was built up over the years, including, for example, two goods motors on the coastal line, open-balcony trailers on the same route, and a number of cars used to operate urban services in some of the smaller Belgian towns like Ostend and Louvain. The last two-axle cars were put into service in 1935, and thereafter the typical SNCV car was the bogie Standard. These long double-ended vehicles were built first in wood and later in metal, in both motor and trailer versions. Very often when the wooden bodies of older motors were replaced they were thriftily reused for trailers. A few non-standard vehicles, like the single-ended Braine-le-Comte cars, were produced, and some of the Standards were later modified, like the Eugies cars which were fitted with pneumatically-operated sliding doors for one-man services. The final development of the SNCV electric fleet came

Above Vicinal bogie motor class N 10427 at a passing loop in Itterbeek, near Brussels. Note the automatic light signals which protect single-line sections

with the N class motors, a more streamlined car which was developed during and after the war. Fitted with two 85hp motors, they have a top speed of 44mph, and can carry 100 passengers, 33 of them seated. Later on similar bodies were fitted to reconditioned Standard cars, these being known as type S, or, in the case of the coastal fleet, type SO. All remaining services are now operated by such cars, together with a number of Standard trailers, and there is in fact a surplus of modern motors—some have been exported to Gijon in Spain, and some class N motors have been turned into trailers for the main lines from Ostend. As at 31 December 1971 the SNCV owned 219 motors, 197 trailers, 16 *autorails*, 6 locomotives, and 10 works cars.

As was stated at the beginning of this chapter, certain European lines are better described as interurbans rather than as country tramways. At least part of the NZH would have come into this category, and other examples include the Vienna Lokalbahn to the little town of Baden, Hanover's route to Hildesheim, and the two heavy interurbans from Düsseldorf to Krefeld and Duisburg. At one time there was quite a number of such lines in Europe, distinguished from their country cousins by

Below Two-axle motor car 26 is about to run round its trailer at Hergnies on the Reseau de Valenciennes. Note the small door in the dash, used by the conductor to pass along the train

reserved double track, high speed running and large, heavy bogie cars, commonly known as 'ironclads'. A rigid distinction cannot be drawn, but in practice the difference was usually obvious. In Hanover, for example, the management always regarded the Hildesheim line as something rather special. Its cars had a distinctive red and white livery, and from 1904 an express service was operated with extremely luxurious bogie motors and trailers, incorporating such refinements as upholstered seats, double trolley poles, and large picture windows. It was to be nearly fifty years before the urban lines saw a bogie car. The *Hildesheimer Fliegender* maintained its distinctiveness right up until the end, for in the 1950s a modern three-car set was introduced incorporating a dining car, a feature which is still to be found on the Düsseldorf-Duisburg route in the Ruhr. Route 11 was also the testing ground for bogie motor 711, which was rebuilt in the Hanover workshops from a trailer in 1950 as a prototype for the later *Grossraumwagen* of which the city was one of the pioneers. The two Düsseldorf routes were once rather similar, but they have now been modernised with new articulated cars, which makes them almost indistinguishable from the urban systems in the area. Probably this will be what will happen to most such routes which survive, at least until they áre upgraded into rapid-transit lines, which is the intention in the case of the Düsseldorf interurbans.

There are, of course, a great many more past and present rural and interurban lines which could have been mentioned—the assorted lines of Stern und Hafferl or the Stubaitalbahn in Austria; the numerous Swiss light railways, which are somewhere between a railway and a tramway; the Glenelg line in Adelaide, the only interurban in Australasia, and the city's last surviving tramway; the Koln-Bonner Eisenbahn, more a light railway than a tramway—but space forbids. One omission, that of Great Britain, must be explained. There were in fact very few rural or interurban tramways in the United Kingdom. There was a number of roadside steam lines in Ireland, and one or two on the mainland, the most long-lived of these being the Wantage tramway. There were also a few electric lines, including some pioneer ones already mentioned in Ireland, the Manx Electric, the railway-owned Grimsby and Immingham Light Railway, the Blackpool and Fleetwood Tramroad, the Kinver Light Railway and the Llandudno and Colwyn Bay. Most of these seem to have earned their living, and in

Above Hildesheimer Strasse, Hanover, in 1958 with heavy interurban motor 710, built in 1927, going out to Sarstedt on the truncated route 11

two cases survived, because of their tourist potential, and most of them too followed interurban practice with long stretches of roadside or reserved track and fleets of single-deck bogie cars. Only one or two lines were anything like the European rural tramway, one of these being the Burton and Ashby Light Railway, which ran along country roads between Burton, Ashby and Church Gresley. It was really only a device by the Midland Railway to forestall competition, and it closed after only twenty-one years.

Such lines were never the pervasive influence in England which they were on the continent, and even there the true rural tramway has almost disappeared, it functions taken over by the bus and the lorry. The great exception to this rule is Eastern Europe, where tramways are not subject to competition from the bus and the private car in quite the same way as they are in the West. Even there some country tramways, like those around Lodz in Poland, are now being closed, but others, like the extensive 'Vicinal' networks around Warsaw and Budapest, are being modernised. And even quite minor rural lines survive, and by dint of buying secondhand cars or rebuilding existing ones contrive to keep services going. One of the most remarkable instances of this is the Schöneiche line near Berlin which has rebuilt or purchased an assortment of bogie motor-trailer sets, each of which is painted in a contrasting livery in colours which include red, cream, yellow, green and blue! There are two other country routes in the environs of East Berlin, and all of them connect stations on the S-Bahn network with rural communities, some of them, such as Woltersdorf, very small ones. Two of the most scenic lines are to be found in the Dresden area; one, a metre gauge branch of the city system, operating little green and cream cars up a pretty valley from Niedersedlitz to Kreischa, and the other up the Elbe at Bad Schandau, a noted beauty spot, where the trams run a few kilometres up into the hills through the woods. Dresden has recently obtained and regauged some post-war cars for the Kreischa route, but the Bad Schandau line still uses clerestory stock dating from 1927, which with its immaculate yellow and white paintwork and varnished interiors is an operating museum piece. A few similar lines have survived in the West, particularly in Austria, and others have become commuter lines, whilst some of the interurban routes are likely to be caught up in the present fashion for rapid transit. Whatever happens to its remnants, though, the rural tramway belongs to a past age in common with the American interurban.

CHAPTER SIX

MODERNISATION

DURING the first quarter of the twentieth century the electric tramcar became an accepted feature of the towns and cities of the developed world, and with its rails and wires, its solidity and longevity—forty or fifty years service being by no means unusual—it gave, and still gives, a curious impression of permanence. The tramcar's everlasting Edwardian summer was however to be rudely shattered by the motor vehicle, which over the decades has caused the abandonment of many, perhaps the majority of tramways, and forced those that remain to change out of all recognition. The changes that have brought the tramcar from the standard era into that of rapid transit can usefully be divided into two stages. In the first, which began in the late twenties and which affected most parts of the world, the emphasis was on improving passenger comfort and service speed in order to compete with motor and trolley buses, and to a lesser extent with the private car; an aim which was achieved largely, though not exclusively, by the improvement of the tramcar itself, either by modernising old cars or by building new ones, which varied from the traditional to the extremely advanced. Only the first of these processes was carried out on any scale, because for a variety of reasons few countries found it possible to carry through a really far-reaching modernisation of their tramways in the 1930s.

Those tramways which survived to enter the second stage, which may be dated from the 1950s, have been the subject of a radical reappraisal of the whole concept of the tramway—from the vehicles, via such things as fare collection, to the right of way—first in competition with the private car, and then in response to the need for a viable form of urban transport to supplement or even replace it. This process, which to date has been largely confined to Europe, has been on a much wider scale than previous modernisations, in that it has affected a majority of existing tramways rather than a minority, and has resulted in far more dramatic changes, producing what is in effect a new form of transport—the rapid tramway.

The distinction between first and second stage modernisation cannot be drawn too rigidly, either chronologically or technologically, because whilst some tramways, such as many of the smaller East German systems, are only now in the first stage, many if not all of the features of the second stage, like automatic control or the use of subways, were anticipated in the first or even earlier. The difference between the two stages lies in the fact that certain innovations—such as the articulated car—have been developed on a far wider scale than hithero, whilst a great number of improvements previously only found in isolation have been applied in conjunction to revolutionise the tramway in Europe and from there those in the rest of the world.

The subject of this chapter is the first stage of development, which took place within the same broad geographical divisions as were defined during the standard era, namely Britain, Europe and North America. In the case of the United Kingdom competition from the by-now reliable and comfortable motor and trolley buses was becoming quite intense by the end of the twenties, and unfavourable comparisons were being drawn between these and the trams on grounds of comfort, speed and the cost of permanent way, amongst other things. Trams were also being blamed for causing congestion through having to load in the middle of the road, and the disadvantages of their inflexible route pattern were being canvassed. Several tramway systems, such as Hastings, Ipswich, the Potteries and Wolverhampton, had already closed, though most of them were only small. In the case of the larger systems the capital tied up in tramways was too great for them to contemplate abandonment at this early stage, and most of them made some effort to speed up their services and make them more attractive to the passenger, although the very amount of capital involved made full-scale modernisation something which only the largest or the most resolute systems could envisage. The majority of tramway undertakings, however, attempted to modernise their old standard cars with such features as upholstered seats and new trucks, high speed motors, and air brakes, which permitted more rapid acceleration and deceleration. The final phase in the development of the Glasgow Standards is a case in point, another Scottish example being afforded by Aberdeen, which modernised its older cars from 1927, all being fitted with Peckham P35 trucks, and many with air brakes, new controllers and more powerful motors. An illustration of the success of such a policy is provided by the LUT, which saw its traffic receipts on the Uxbridge Road line rise from 1s (5p) to 1s.8d (8½p) per mile soon after the introduction of modernised trams with upholstered seats in 1928. In other cases, however, very little was done. Hull, for example, bought no new cars after 1914, with one exception, and never even got round to fully-enclosing all its existing fleet, which received no major mechanical improvements apart from the fitting of a few secondhand trucks in 1933.

By this date Hull's tramways were already being dismembered and would have disappeared entirely within a decade had it not been for the outbreak of war. But in those places where total abandonment was not being contemplated the refurbishment of older cars was insufficient to maintain existing services, let alone extend them into the new suburbs which were springing up on the outskirts of the larger cities. Most of the new trams built around this period looked fairly traditional as far as the outline of the body was concerned, and were not radically different from the rebuilt standards operating in, for example, Glasgow, the only thing being that the latest mechanical and electrical improvements were built into these trams instead of having been added in successive rebuildings. For instance, Aberdeen purchased a series of 12 cars fitted with high power motors and air brakes in 1929, but externally these were virtually indistinguishable from earlier vehicles. However more modern methods of construction involving metal panels on a wooden frame instead of wood throughout were gradually coming into vogue, which meant that new cars could be both lighter and stronger at the same time, and could also incorporate certain variations of styling, which though relatively minor in themselves gave the cars a more modern and attractive appearance. Thus some of the trams of this vintage, such as the later Sheffield Standards, dispensed with the old inward-curving rocker panels in favour of straight sides, whilst a number of cars, such as the Sheffield 1936 series and the Manchester Pilchers, were built with domed roofs, which added quite a touch of distinction to an otherwise fairly orthodox design. An excellent example of the sort of progress made in the early thirties is afforded by Leeds, whose Horsfield cars, named like many others after the general manager of the day, provided a marked contrast with the earlier Pivotal series, which, trucks apart, were of an extremely traditional design. The Horsfields, which were built in 1930–1, were given a much neater appearance by the ommission of the rocker panels and of the continuous line of quarter lights along the top deck characteristic of the older cars, whose angular lines were softened by the use of curved glass at the ends. Comfortable two-and-one seats were provided on both decks, and platform doors were added later on. Basically though this generation of cars, both new and rebuilt, differed from their predecessors not in appearance but in performance and comfort, a result which was achieved by a combination of improvements such as lighter materials, longer trucks with better riding qualities, high speed motors, more effective brakes and better seating, all of which represented developments of existing technology rather than any radical innovations.

Quite a few experiments in tramcar design were, however, made during the twenties and thirties. Several undertakings toyed with the idea of bogie single-deckers on the American pattern. Liverpool, for example, built a clerestory-roofed 44-seater in 1929 with the intention of operating it through the Mersey Tunnel, but after this scheme fell through the car was withdrawn and the design discarded in favour of modern double-deckers, a policy which was also followed in Glasgow, where an experimental high-speed single-decker had been built in 1926. In another case, that of Bradford, single-deckers appeared attractive because the Board of Trade would not normally permit fully-enclosed single-truck double-deckers on narrow gauge systems, the Bradford gauge being 4ft. Actually one or two such cars were permitted on some small Lancashire systems, but Bradford had to retain its open balconies right up to the end of tramway operation in 1950, as the bogie single-decker had been withdrawn in 1931 after the decision to replace the tramways by trolleybuses. A much later single-deck experiment took place in Leeds in 1953–4 when three cars were built as prototypes for a new fleet. One was technically a rebuild of an ex-Sunderland car, but the others were built by the local firm of C. H. Roe in order to test the relative merits of two rival systems of control, each car being fitted with a different mechanism—601 with conventional remote control equipment and 602 with automatic control. Unfortunately the decision to abandon Leeds tramways was taken almost at the same time, and all three cars had very short working lives.

A few other towns produced single specimens of modern cars, which though no doubt intended to be the precursors of a new fleet, in fact turned out to be unique, having been overtaken by political decisions to abandon the tramways. One such was LCC 1, which was built in 1932 as the prototype for a series to replace London's older trams, but when the London Passenger Transport Board took over in 1933 it decided upon a policy of trolleybus replacement, and no more were built. This was a bogie car, fully-enclosed, with platform doors, separate driver's cabs and a high standard of comfort, and after running in London for a number of years it was eventually sold to Leeds.

In other cases experimental tramcars were followed by production batches, which, when coupled with rebuilt stock, succeeded in revitalising the fleets concerned for a further twenty to thirty years service. To the passenger the most obvious feature of most of these new cars was their streamlined bodywork, usually of all-metal construction with consequent savings in weight. The passenger might also have noticed the smoother acceleration provided by the latest control mechanisms, and certainly would have remarked upon the high standard of comfort afforded by these new trams. In some cases more-or-less conventional four-wheelers were produced with the new-style bodies, examples being the Belfast McCrearies, of composite construction and dating from 1935, and the Sheffield streamliners, which were the last new double-deckers to be built in Britain after the war. One of the first modern cars to be produced in any quantity were the Felthams which were put into service on the London company lines from 1931. These long maximum-traction bogie cars were based on no less than five prototypes and incorporated most of the improvements currently available, such as lightweight prefabricated bodywork, air and magnetic brakes, roller bearings, platform doors, straight stairs, unobstructed saloons without bulkheads, front exit and separate motormen's cabs. Conventional controllers were fitted, but the motors provided very good acceleration. Most of the cars, which had a very distinctive appearance with their great length and protruding cabs, ended their days in service in Leeds.

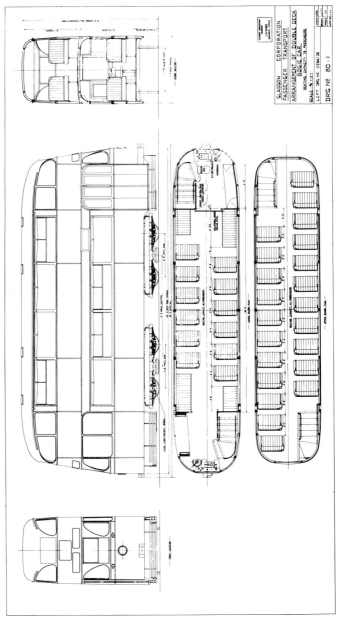

A Green Goddess bogie streamliner, originally built for Liverpool and later sold to Glasgow. This is one of the batch with EMB lightweight bogies transferred in 1954 *[Greater Glasgow PTE*

One of the most remarkable programmes of renewal took place in the relatively small town of Blackpool, which purchased a total of 104 new streamlined trams between 1933 and 1938. The majority were enclosed single-deckers, but there were also 27 double-deckers, some of which originally had open tops, and 12 open single-deckers for summer traffic. Most of these cars are still in service, although many have been rebuilt once or even twice in the course of their lives. Ten single-deck rail-coaches have, for example, been reconstructed to form towing cars for ten new trailers purchased in 1960, and a number of other cars have recently re-entered service as one-man trams with completely restyled bodies and a new livery of maroon and yellow to replace the standard green and cream. The most interesting, and in the last analysis least successful post-war experiment in Blackpool was the development of the sophisticated control mechanism known as VAMBAC. The basic principle of this was that the driver selected a rate of acceleration or braking which was automatically and smoothly achieved by a control unit mounted on the roof. One car was experimentally fitted with the new equipment in 1946, and was so successful that 12 other cars, nos 10–21 of 1939—were similarly adapted for service on the Marton route. They were followed by 25 entirely new Coronation cars in 1952–3, but it was found that the complex Vambac equipment often gave trouble, whilst the high speeds which it was designed to achieve were simply not possible when inter-running with older cars. Hence the Coronations were first modified to reduce their top speed by about 20mph, and later had their Vambac units replaced by surplus conventional controllers; most of them have now joined the Marton Vambacs in the scrapyard, leaving Blackpool's one remaining tram service, the Promenade line to Fleetwood, to the older streamliners.

Rather more suited to British conditions was the simpler electro-pneumatic remote control system, which was used on quite a number of cars such as the Glasgow Coronations, mostly built between 1937 and 1941, the later Cunarders of postwar vintage, and Liverpool's Green Goddess bogie streamliners, some of which also ended up in Glasgow. Remote control was necessary because the new high-powered cars, often with four motors, needed very heavy switch gear to cope with the high currents employed. To ease the motorman's task this switchgear was operated by a low voltage control circuit, which meant that the driver

Above One of Blackpool's less successful experiments was this 1935 railcoach, rebuilt with plastic panels which were later found to warp badly. The scene is the Promenade in 1972

was actually controlling the tram indirectly through this equipment, which was usually fitted in a cupboard under the stairs. Over 250 of the two Glasgow types were eventually produced, and 213 of the Liverpool bogies, which were later joined by a series of 100 single-truck streamliners known as Baby Grands. Together they formed the finest tramcars ever produced in quantity in Great Britain. They included such features as folding platform doors, at a time when buses all had open rear platforms, effective heating derived from the control resistances, and leather seats. The prewar Glasgow cars, and some of the Liverpool bogies, were fitted with the latest lightweight trucks, and the postwar Cunarders, or Coronation Mark IIs, with the newer inside-frame bogies derived from American practice and designed to give a smoother and quieter ride—though in practice they tended to roll badly. Certainly, however, in 1939 these two cities possessed some of the best tramcars to be found in the whole continent of Europe—the only trouble was that there were not enough of them and Glasgow, for example, had to postpone and then finally abandon its plans to purchase 700 similar cars to renew the rest of its fleet.

Although the main emphasis of this period was on the tramcar itself, certain ancillary features were also improved, notably the track. In order to reduce noise thermit welding of joints became standard on most tramways, and some systems, led by Leeds, introduced junctions with raised grooves, which had the effect of making cars run through on their flanges, for the same purpose. Tramway services were also speeded up by the transfer of tracks from the street to reservations, either beside or in the centre of the road or on private right-of-way. The first such lines had been laid before World War I in, for example, Birmingham and Southend in 1913 and in Liverpool in the following year, but further development was held up until after the war. Then considerable mileages of sleeper track were laid in such cities as Birmingham, Leeds and Liverpool, in many cases being new extensions to postwar housing developments, the Middleton Light Railway in Leeds, opened in 1925, being a good example. Liverpool eventually had a total of nearly 28 miles on reservation, and many other systems, large and small, had at least some, ranging from Huddersfield's $\frac{3}{4}$ mile through the woods at Fixby to Blackpool's 10-mile Promenade line, whose almost total segregation is the main reason for its survival.

The overhead also received attention during the thirties, the most obvious feature being the adoption of the Fischer bow collector in place of the traditional trolley pole in certain towns, such as Aberdeen, Glasgow and Leeds. These obviously eliminated dewirements and made reversal easier, but they were also found to minimise wear on the trolley wire, with a consequent saving in expensive copper. Pantographs were never popular in the United Kingdom, Sunderland and the Swansea and Mumbles line being about the only examples of their use.

However, despite all the improvements which had been made, it was becoming clear by the end of the decade that it was a case of too little and too late. After all, of the 14,000 tramcars running in 1930 less than 1,000 had been replaced by really modern vehicles, and in almost every individual case the majority of the fleet was ageing or obsolete. To this was added the weight of government opinion, which was firmly against the tram, and which naturally affected the decisions of the remaining tramway strongholds. By the time war broke out, in fact, most of the

Below   Glasgow Cunarder 1321, built 1950, poses in Balmoral Street, Scotstoun, a short-working point for route 26, in September 1961

smaller systems had already succumbed and many of the larger ones had made considerable progress with tramway abandonment, largely because the cost of track and fleet renewal was felt to be prohibitive. It was only wartime conditions which kept some systems going as long as they did, and some of them, such as Hull and Plymouth, closed as soon as the war was over, while others, such as London, only ran until replacement buses were available. The remaining systems, notably Aberdeen, Edinburgh, Glasgow, Leeds, Liverpool, Sheffield and Sunderland, carrried on as long as they could, but with a majority of older cars and the prohibitive costs of obtaining new ones—which anyway no-one was any longer really equipped to build—the eventual decision to abandon was almost inevitable. Glasgow was the last city tramway to close, in 1962, and that left Blackpool as Britain's only remaining urban electric tramway system—truly a case of 'the last shall be first and the first last'.

European tramways during the interwar years followed the same policies of gradual renewal and replacement as those in Britain, though naturally beginning as they did with a very different type of tramcar, the actual results were rather dissimilar, even though the techniques employed, such as metal bodywork and improved electrical and mechanical equipment, were not. A major difference between Britain and Europe, though, was that in the latter very few tramways were closed during this period, with the exception of those in France, where a policy of abandonment almost more drastic than that in the United Kingdom was adopted—the last tram ran in Paris, for example, as early as 1938. But apart from that it was usually only the smaller systems, such as the single route at Enschede, Holland, which closed in 1933, or the Meissen system, near Dresden, which lost its passenger service in 1936, which were abandoned. Of those systems which remained, many pursued the modernisation of their older cars with vigour. The example of Copenhagen has already been quoted, and others included Barcelona, where the bodies of most cars were renovated during the 1920s, and Brussels, where the existing fleet was reconstructed to produce about 800 standard two-axle cars, the last of which has only recently been withdrawn. Of typically Belgian appearance, with angular cream-painted bodies, the most obviously modern feature about these cars was the absence of a clerestory, at least until they were further modernised in 1948–9 with air-operated folding doors and seated conductor. Not every system, however, either needed to or was able to carry out a full scale programme of renewal. This naturally included many of the smaller places, but also some of the larger, like Hanover, which had a number of fairly modern wooden-bodied standards built in the 1920s, and at the end of that decade took delivery of almost a hundred new metal-bodied cars, which meant that the need for rebuilding the older trams did not arise until much later. When it did, it was already too late, for after the trial modernisation of a wooden motor car with lengthened platforms, barrel roof etc, the war stopped all further progress and, as in many other cities, ensured the survival of the old clerestory-roofed cars for many years after that.

Most of the new cars built during this period followed the well-tried European two-axle design, though naturally incorporating the latest improvements, the most notable of which was the substitution of steel for wooden bodywork. This enabled the old-fashioned clerestory to be discarded in favour of a domed roof, a typical example of the style being the Berlin types 24 and 25, of which just over 1,300 were built in the mid-twenties. Most countries evolved similar cars during the same period, for instance the Russian all-steel four-wheelers produced from 1926, a particularly creditable achievement when one realises that most tramway systems had completely collapsed during the Revolution and had lost almost half their rolling stock. Passenger comfort also received attention, although the transverse upholstered seats to be found on the Frankfurt type F—an all-steel series built in 1925–6—were never as common on the continent as elsewhere. Mechanical improvements related mainly to the motors, which were speeded up, and to new types of brakes, such as magnetic and rheostatic, which enabled higher service speeds to be maintained.

Although the majority of cars followed the normal end-platform design, centre entrances had a vogue in certain cities, such as Paris, where the fleet was standardised on this pattern during the twenties, and Berlin, where about 400 motors were in service by the time war broke out. Some of these have been converted to works cars of class 721 and can still be seen in the East German capital in the departmental livery of green and cream. Another departure from the norm was brought about by the perennial problem of getting two-axle cars around corners, a difficulty which was overcome on the continent rather better than it was anywhere else. The solution was the same as that pioneered by Cleminson with his radial-axle horse car—that is, a six wheel truck in which the two outer pairs of wheels were allowed to turn freely to meet curves, but were then restored to parallelism by the action of the central 'link-axle'. It was the absence of the third pair of wheels which caused the pivotal trucks used in Leeds to fail to return to the straight and narrow after rounding a curve, with unfortunate results on both the track and the passengers; eventually these trucks had to be locked in the parallel position. The same happened to 17 very similar sets of trucks supplied to the German town of Plauen in 1905, and it was soon realised by European tramway engineers that the difficulties inherent in the pivotal design could swiftly be solved by the addition of the third axle. However three-axle cars found no favour in either America or Britain, although London United had experimented with a Barber six-wheel truck in 1909, and at least one open-sided six-wheeler was running in Milwaukee in the early years of the century. In Europe though the six-wheel truck provided bogie riding qualities at the cost of standard two-motor equipment, and a great number of them have been built. For instance the greater part of the Ghent fleet until very recently consisted of 105 clerestory six-wheel motors, and Basle, which built two traditionally-styled three-axle motors in the thirties, had a sizeable fleet of trailers of a rather more modern design. Another example was the Lille 700 series motors, which incorporated modern features such as cardan shaft drive and regenerative braking. These, despite their good riding qualities, were withdrawn in 1962 a little in advance of the closure of the Lille town system because of the expense of maintenance—a common complaint with six-wheelers which mitigated against their more general acceptance.

Another way of bringing a fleet up-to-date, at least outwardly, was to fit new metal bodies to the underframes of old standard cars, a pre-war example being afforded by the Budapest class FM1, which after starting life with bogies in 1897 were first rebuilt with two-axles and then given new steel-framed bodies in 1938, which did not leave much of the original cars! This was about the ultimate in tramcar rebuilding, however, and the process could not go on for ever, quite apart from the fact that such rebuilt cars did not have the performance to match their modernised exteriors. Hence at about the same time a number of undertakings were involved in the design and testing of really modern two-axle trams intended to be the standard cars of the future. In 1935, for instance, Dusseldorf introduced the prototype of the later *Niederflur*, or low-platform,

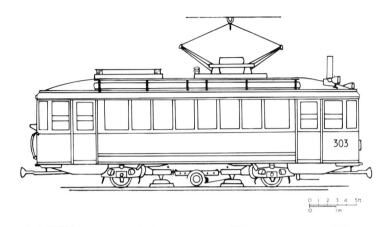

Basle three-axle motor car No 303 was built in 1935, one of only two such cars in the fleet. It was a particularly large example of a six-wheel car, with a total capacity of 80 passengers, and it illustrates clearly the principle of the linked three-axle truck   [*P. N. C. Cooke*

design, of which over 100 motors and trailers were built for the Rheinbahn itself, and several for other German cities, such as Mulheim and Neuss. The distinguishing feature of these cars was the very low floor, which was achieved by a special design of truck and, on the motors, by the use of very small yet powerful motors. Two cars which never got further than the prototype stage were a streamlined motor and trailer built for Hanover in 1938. The body style was very like the contemporary American PCC, and the cars were far in advance of most German trams of the day, with reversible upholstered seats, a control lever, low voltage equipment and a loudspeaker to announce the stopping places. Unfortunately the war halted any further development of this design, although Hanover did obtain 15 other new cars from the firm of Credé during the war. The undertaking also obtained ten trailers of the *Einheitswagen* (ESW) type, which had actually been intended for Berlin, where 20 were put into service in 1942. These again had reversible upholstered seats, but although intended at the time to be the future

German standard tram, wartime conditions brought production to a halt before long.

Parallel with the introduction of new types of two-axle tram, renewed interest was being shown on the continent in the bogie car, which until then had been very much the exception rather than the rule. One of the first really large fleets to go into service—500 motors for Milan built by Italian firms in 1928–30—were modelled on the American Peter Witt design, and were perhaps the most successful cars of their generation, having formed the backbone of the Milan fleet right up until the present day and outlived most of their contemporaries and many later models. Such cars were also used in Turin, and Italian systems as a whole were far in advance of the rest of Europe in the introduction of bogie cars. For instance Genoa's 700 class dated from 1931, and although of somewhat archaic appearance, they were equipped with a device still thought modern in the 1960s—namely two body-mounted motors driving both axles of each bogie via cardan shafts which, in the same way as maximum

Below   One of Oslo's prewar streamliners ad Marjorstua depot before the class was transferred to work the suburban route to Jar [*Oslo Sporveier*

traction trucks, meant that only two motors instead of the usual four were needed. The later 900 series, built in 1939–40, were typical examples of a more modern type of tram found in several Italian cities such as Milan, Rome and Turin. These had streamlined bodies, automatic control equipment, and modern bogies with excellent riding characteristics, and although the Genoa cars have now been withdrawn others of the type are still in service in other cities. Such was the momentum of tramway modernisation achieved in Italy that progress continued to be made until well into the war—for instance, both Genoa and Milan introduced a small group of articulated cars in 1942, following the example set by Rome in 1939, and in the same year, 1942, Turin put its first PCC car into service, both of which developments will be covered more fully below.

Things were otherwise in Germany, where the preparation for and prosecution of the war took a greater share of public resources, and where also the tradition of two-axle trams was stronger. The most notable pre-war bogie cars were the Dresden *Grosshechtwagen*, or large pike cars, so described because of their sharply-pointed prows. 33 of the class were built between 1930 and 1933. They had upholstered seats for 36 and room for 76 standing, and were exceptionally powerful with 4×55k W motors and a top speed of 60 km/h, which enabled them to cope with the extremely hilly route to Bühlau on which they spent most of their working lives; 48 similar two-axle cars, known as the *Kleinhechtwagen*, were also built, but were rather too light to prove as successful as the bogies. Both classes have now been withdrawn apart from a few on works duties. They lasted much longer, though, than the double-ended bogie motors built for Essen in 1933–40. Some were destroyed in the war, but even though the 12 which remained were of a very handsome streamlined design, they had not been built very well and were soon either withdrawn or converted to trailers.

The 1930s, of course, with their economic and political crises, were not the best time to be considering tramway modernisation, and many plans had to be curtailed. For instance Copenhagen had designed and built a prototype bogie motor and trailer set in 1930 with the intention of adding 30 to the fleet each year. In the event only 118 motors and 83 trailers had been delivered by 1941, when construction ceased, but even so the result was a very fine series of cars, a few of which survived until the system closed in 1972. There was nothing especially remarkable about these all-steel cars, unless it was the particularly generous width of the saloon windows, but they always looked exceptionally smart. Indeed the Copenhagen system was always renowned for the condition of its fleet, and even the postwar articulated cars, though no different from anyone else's, always contrived to look that bit more elegant. Developments in other countries included the production of a standard all-steel bogie in Russia from 1935, an improved version of which appeared in 1938; the introduction of a large fleet of centre-entrance cars in Rotterdam; and the delivery of the small 5000 class to Brussels in 1935. But in almost every case the outbreak of war slowed down and eventually stopped all progress.

The only exceptions to this were the neutral countries, in effect Sweden and Switzerland, as Spanish tramways were still recovering from the effects of the Civil War. Switzerland, rather oddly for a country which is so politically fragmented, had set about designing a

Below An offside view of one of Copenhagen's prewar bogies in the Kongens Nytorv, showing the lights and plaques used as part of the route-colour system [*J. J. Richardson*

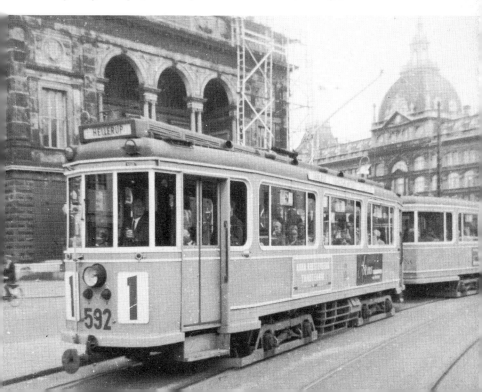

Swiss standard bogie tram in the mid-thirties, and the first had appeared in 1937 for use on the rural Biel-Meinisberg line, from which it was later transferred to Lugano. These cars, built as both motors and trailers, are single-ended and have a fairly severe styling with particularly sharp ends to avoid fouling the opposite track at curves. Because of their simple design, however, they have worn well and still look up-to-date. Their control mechanism and bogies are similar to contemporary American PCC design, although of Swiss manufacture. One of the first major systems to use them was Zurich, which took delivery of its first 38 motors between 1940 and 1946. The first trailers were put into service in 1945, and since then a fleet of over 100 motors and 75 trailers has been built up. The other major Swiss system, Basle, did not begin using Standard cars until 1947, when the first trailers were delivered, but now has a total of 79 motors and 105 trailers, the odd number in each case being accounted for by the existence of an earlier experimental vehicle. The design of the standard car has naturally evolved over the years, and both cities have experimented with a lightweight version, the four-motor Zurich design, of which 53 were built, proving more successful than the Basle 'ultra-light' motor, which had only one powered bogie and two motors. At 12 tonnes this weighed far less than the average 20 tonnes of the earlier models, and 3 tonnes less even than the Zurich cars, but only three were ever built. The advantage, of course, is that a saving can be made in power consumption, and most of the Zurich lightweight cars, for example, have 4x65hp motors as opposed to the more normal 4x85hp.

In Sweden, the other major neutral power, there was no actual standard design, although modern Swedish trams have always looked remarkably like each other, most of them having slightly swept-back flat fronts as opposed to the more normal pointed or curved prow. To take one example, Gothenburg built a prototype bogie car for urban service in 1937. This was single-ended and designed for passenger flow, and experience with it led to an order for 15 motors of type M22 delivered in 1943–44. This was followed by a postwar order for 63 motors of type M23 and 70 trailers of type S27, and all further cars have been of the bogie pattern. Most other Swedish systems, such as Malmo and Stockholm, re-equipped at least part of their fleet with similar cars, although Gothenburg was alone in having tracks wide enough apart to permit cars with a row of double-seats on both sides of the gangway, which may be

Above *Verbandstyp* motor 194, ex-Lübeck, in the Berliner Platz, Kiel, as adapted for one-man service on the now-closed route 2

one reason why the tram has retained its popularity there almost alone amongst Swedish cities.

The ability of the neutral powers to initiate and carry through programmes of tramway modernisation during and immediately after the war was in marked contrast to the situation pertaining in the rest of Europe. An immediate effect of the outbreak of war was a vast increase in tramway traffic resulting from the restrictions on motor transport—in Copenhagen, for example, the annual passenger total rose by 20 million between 1939 and 1942. At the same time the ability of undertakings to cope was reduced by the shelving of modernisation plans, by lack of maintenance and, later on, by war damage. As the war went on Germany began 'borrowing' trams from occupied territory, mainly the Low Countries, which naturally made matters there even worse. Denmark, regarded by the Germans as a model protectorate, was one exception to this policy, and in 1942 the Kobenhavns Sporveje was even able to begin building a series of two-axle motors and trailers using parts from scrapped cars. These were austerity versions of the earlier bogies, and production continued until 1947, when over 100 of the class were in service. This example is typical of the retrograde effect which the war had on tramcar design, forcing undertakings to revert to cheap two-axle cars instead of the more expensive bogies. In Germany itself allied air raids were beginning to take an increasing toll of rolling stock by the 1940s, and a very basic *Kriegsstrassenbahnwagen* (KSW) was rushed into service in 1944, a total of 244 motors and 409 trailers being built before production ceased about 1950. These cars were very distinctive, with three large saloon windows, a minumum of seating, short trucks and long, overhanging platforms. Some ended up in Poland, where the design was improved to form the standard postwar tramcar, the class N. Both Germany and its eastern neighbours built large numbers of two-axle cars after the war to replace destroyed or damaged vehicles as quickly as possible. As an indication of the scale of the problem, the Dresden raids of 13–14 February 1945 left 185 trams totally destroyed and 303 damaged to a greater or lesser extent, while 92km of overhead had been brought down and the inner city network rendered totally unusable.* In many cases it was possible to provide new bodies for war-damaged trams, and this was done in both West and East Germany. The Western *Aufbau*—rebuilt—cars had four-window saloons and neat tapered ends, and most of them were two-axle, although a few three-axle and bogie versions were produced as well. A later development of the same design was the *Verbandstyp*, in this case with new trucks as well as bodies, and with a pleasing streamlined appearance. Frankfurt is an example of a system which has operated all three types of car, most of which have now been withdrawn or, in the case of some other systems, rebuilt. In East Germany, once the *Aufbau* stage was over, the two basic types of post-war cars have been the LOWA, an all-steel car with a rather distinctive bulge at the waist, and the Gotha T57, of which over 2,000 were produced from 1957, the majority of them being exported to the Soviet Union. Recently a large number of older cars have been rebodied in the same style, most of them for Berlin, which now uses only these *Rekowagen* and

---

* Irving D. *The Destruction of Dresden* (1971)

a few score modern bogies—actually the entire East German production, which was halted in favour of Czechoslovakia, which now supplies nearly all of East Germany's tramcars. The Communist countries generally, and East Germany in particular, have relied upon two-axle cars for longer than western tramways, and indeed it is only now that the larger East German tramways are beginning to replace them with bogied or articulated cars—which is another story.

So far as the track and overhead was concerned, the most notable change on the continent in this period was the replacement of both trolley poles and bow collectors by pantographs, which are now used almost universally. Ghent was one of the last places in Western Europe to use the old long continental bow collector, while trolley poles are now only to be found in a few places such as Brussels and Milan, where they are gradually being phased out in favour of the latest one-arm pantographs, and Hamburg, where the trams themselves are being run down. In surprising contrast to Great Britain, reserved track was relatively uncommon in Europe before the war, and even double track in the middle of the street, though found in certain cities like Dusseldorf and Cologne, was by no means the rule. Many miles of tramway were still laid in the gutter or alongside the road, and much of this was single track with passing loops, which meant that services were slow and delays more probable. A remaining example of such a line is Ghent's route 20 from Arsenaal to Melle, although this is more rural than many of the prewar German tramways. Improvements to the track itself, at least on the more progressive systems, were not lacking in such matters as raised groove junctions, which were a continental idea, and track welding, but much of it was still laid in sets, which of course inconvenienced other traffic more than it did the trams. Even today cities such as East Berlin and Dresden are engaged in relaying old track, much of it badly sunken, with new concrete paving. It was in fact the destruction caused by the war which gave tramways in Germany in particular the opportunity of providing entirely new double-track layouts and reserved tracks, which are now far more common than they ever were in Britain.

By the same date it was already becoming clear that the American streetcar, with one or two important exceptions, was destined to become a thing of the past. The trends were already visible in the 1920s or even earlier, though it is doubtful whether anyone could then have forseen the extent of the changes in the travelling habits of the public which reduced trolley passengers from 5.8 billion in 1902 to only 1,115 million in 1954, and the number of streetcars to less than 7,000 in the whole of the United States. American street railways were the victims of large-scale public and private motor vehicle competition much earlier than their European counterparts, and partly as a result of this had already gone through most of the stages described above well before 1930. All metal construction, lightweight bodywork, high speed motors—all had been tried, and none had succeeded in arresting the flow of flivvers and motor coaches, which had already swamped the interurban and now seemed poised to overwhelm the city lines also.

So it was that in 1929 25 of the major street railway companies and most of the car and equipment builders banded together in the 'Electric Railway Presidents' Conference Committee' with the intention of designing and producing a modern streetcar capable of competing in terms of speed and comfort with the private automobile, and in addition able to compare favourably with the bus in financial terms. Over one million dollars was spent on fundamental research into streetcar design and into the likes and dislikes of passengers—for instance, into such things as the maximum tolerable rate of acceleration, which turned out to be much higher than anyone had expected. To avoid any danger of simply tinkering with existing trolley design the chief engineer was appointed from outside the industry, and the result—the PCC or 'Presidents' Conference Committee' Car—was indeed something quite out of the ordinary. The streamlined body, though new to American eyes, was not all that revolutionary, being paralleled by, for example, the Blackpool railcoaches or some of the prewar Italian streamliners. The innovations lay in the trucks and the control equipment, which are still used in many of today's modern trams. One of the main features which so astounded contemporary observers when the first prototype was unveiled at the 1934 meeting of the American Transit Association was the uncanny silence of the PCC, which was the result of various improvements to the truck, notably the use of rubber springing and rubber inserts in the wheels, together with new silent gears. This contrasted not only with the old trolleys but also with the latest European designs, such as the Liverpool streamliners and the Milanese bogies, which still made all the usual tramway noises. No other contemporary car, either, could match the

Above Two American PCCs at the portal of the Twin Peaks Tunnel in San Francisco [*San Francisco Municipal Railway*

performance of the PCC, which was not just a matter of high speed—the interurbans had always been capable of that—but of how it was reached. In traditional tramcars power was fed to the motors in, say, eight stages, which naturally made for slow and/or jerky acceleration. The PCC remote control unit, however, provided for over 90 stages, which allowed both swift and smooth acceleration and braking, on the same lines as the later British VAMBAC system. In a PCC the passenger is pressed back into the seat as the car starts, which is not a sensation one often feels in a bus! Other features of the prototype PCC included modern lighting, ventilation and seating, foot control by a seated operator, and air-operated folding doors. No trailers were to be used with PCCs, and most of them were single-ended, with one or two exceptions such as those used in Dallas and on the Pacific Electric.

The prototype car was added to the first production batch of 100 delivered to the Brooklyn-Manhattan Transit Corporation of New York in 1936. The cars proved immediately popular in service, but unfortunately the tide was running too strongly in favour of buses to persuade many operators to change their minds about scrapping the trolleys.

Only 1100 PCCs had been purchased by 1940, and although about 5,000 were eventually delivered to undertakings in the USA and Canada, this was enough only to delay abandonment in most cases, such as Kansas City, Los Angeles and New York, or to maintain services on a limited number of routes in cities like San Francisco and Philadelphia where streetcars were retained.

The majority of American PCCs were manufactured by two companies, the St Louis Car Co and Pullman, with electrical equipment by either Westinghouse or General Electric. Various detail alterations were made to suit individual purchasers—for example a special truck had to be designed for the 3ft 6in gauge Los Angeles system—and certain improvements were made over time to both the body and the equipment. The earliest cars had rather small windows through which it was quite impossible for standing passengers to see. So later models had a row of little 'standee' windows added above these, which cured that problem, although it made the cars much uglier to look at. The latest Boston series, dating from 1951 and very nearly the last built in North America, have what are described as 'picture windows', which are rather longer than the old style, but no higher, meaning that standee windows are still necessary. Later PCCs also had the air-operated brakes, door mechanism etc replaced by all-electric equipment. The Los Angeles fleet, for example, consisted of 25 air-brake cars dating from 1937–44 and 40 all-electric cars delivered in 1948. The earlier series were also somewhat smaller, although, at 61, they seated three more than the later cars. The only other major change was the fitting of equipment for multiple-unit operation on the cars belonging to some systems. All the Boston fleet, for instance, with the exception of 17 ex-Dallas double-enders, are so fitted, as are some of the Toronto cars, the latter being publicised at the time as 'streamliners on the double', the claimed advantage being that they could get through traffic lights more quickly than single units. Toronto, incidentally, though alone amongst Canadian systems in adopting the PCC, ended up with the largest fleet on the continent—a total of 714 in 1953, many of which were purchased second-hand from American systems. Later 30 more PCCs were acquired from Kansas City, which also sold 40 to Philadelphia, and 10 to Tampico in Mexico, where the capital, Mexico City, has a much larger fleet of ex-American PCCs. Kansas City also disposed of 75 sets of trucks and equipment to Brussels, which rebuilt them with new European-style bodies. Most other remaining American systems also have some secondhand cars amongst their fleet. San Francisco, for example, has quite a number from St Louis, many of which were leased rather than bought owing to peculiar local restrictions on the Municipal Railway.

At the same time as the PCCs were introduced a parallel modernisation of older cars was continuing. In Toronto, for instance, all of the steel motor cars were rebuilt for 'PAY-ENTER' (PAYE) operation, a system which was becoming almost universal on the North American continent. Other improvements made to these cars included leather upholstered foam rubber seats, non-skid linoleum flooring, and forced-air electric heating. The opening of the subway system during the 1950s caused the withdrawal of the last of these Peter Witt cars, although oddly enough two have only recently been refurbished to provide a tourist service, so adding Toronto to the select list of cities such as Copenhagen, Dresden and Montreal which have operated sightseeing trams. Track and overhead were also being improved at the same time as the modernisation of the fleets. In Toronto thermit welding is now standard, a system which not only reduces noise at the rail joints, but also results in stronger track with better electrical conductivity. Other developments included the provision of loops to eliminate awkward reversing movements and the fitting of electrically operated points instead of the old hand-operated variety—a change which was taking place in Britain and Europe as well. Rather an anachronism to European eyes is the trolley pole which is still used on all existing American systems, with the exception of the new Fort Worth line, which provides one of the few examples of the use of the pantograph.

Of the nine or ten American systems which remain today, all except one, New Orleans, are operated solely by PCC cars. And the achievement of the PCC has been to keep at least part of these systems intact until a time when public opinion is once again running in favour of railed transport, and there is opportunity for them to be integrated into a really modern transit system. The achievement is not that of the PCC alone, however, for virtually every one of the remaining systems, which were by no means unique in using PCCs, owes its survival to the fact that some or all of its route is segregated from the public highway. Boston, Newark, Philadelphia and the privately-built line at Fort Worth, Texas, have their subways, and San Francisco its tunnels; the Shaker Heights line in Cleveland is entirely on reservation, as is much of the remaining mileage in Pittsburgh. The two other systems are El Paso and Toronto, and the latter, with San Francisco, stands out in being a major city with a majority of its system still on street track. In Toronto streetcar lines serve those parts of the city untouched by the subways, and a recent press release stated that streetcars 'still provide the ideal means of moving people on major surface routes', and are able to cope with traffic flows of up to 9,000 passengers per hour in each direction more efficiently than any alternative mode of transport.

No streetcars have been built in North America for over 20 years, and most of the PCCs are older than that, which means that they are in grave need of replacement. Plans are now well-advanced for the building of a new standard American streetcar, but in the interim many undertakings are rehabilitating their existing PCCs. Pittsburgh, for example, is restoring 70 of its 95 cars to 'like new' condition under its Early Action Programme, whilst Toronto has a similar scheme to renovate about half of its much larger fleet over a five-year period. 50 cars will be completely overhauled each year, and the work includes rewiring, renewing the rear half of the metal roof, installing new wooden floors, re-upholstering the seats, and a new interior colour scheme. The scheme is, however, subject to annual review, and there has recently been some controversy about the future of the Toronto system. At least one of the 11 routes is likely to close, but even so the immediate future of the rest of the system is fairly secure, and tentative plans exist for some quite new light rapid transit lines. As far as the United States is concerned, the most precarious systems are New Orleans, which has no modern cars, and Pittsburgh, where the few remaining streetcars face competition from new developments such as busways and the automated Transit Expressway, which is a sort of guided electric bus. Otherwise the remaining American systems are likely to be modernised and retained, perhaps even extended at some future date.

Details of American systems have been brought almost to the present day because, though modern in many respects, they are essentially products of the 1930s. Developments in the rest of the world outside Britain and Europe during this period were broadly similar to those already described, in most cases involving improvements on existing themes rather than anything radically new. South America became almost entirely dependent upon cast-off American stock, whilst the established British tradition in South Afircan tramway circles was continued by johannesburg when it took delivery of about 50 all-metal double-deckers in 1935. In Australia the development of the indiginous drop-centre cars was continued in most cases, perhaps the most handsome design being the prewar Brisbane cars with their domed roofs and sharply tapered ends. The most numerous, though, were the variations on the Melbourne class W built by the undertaking itself from 1923 onwards. The last prewar type embodied such things as improved seating, windows and ceiling, together with power-operated sliding doors.

But despite the fact that many important advances in tramway design and technology were made during the two decades 1930–50, modernisation was generally ineffective. In Britain and North America it failed to stop the gradually accelerating trend towards tramway abandonment, largely because of economic pressures upon operators. Elsewhere it failed to transform the old standard fleets into anything which could be described as truly modern, the reasons for this being both economic and, particularly, political in the shape of World War II. In a few cases, however, such as Italy, Sweden and Switzerland, some progress was made, and it was obvious that the future, if there was to be one, lay in Europe where the majority of existing tramways were to be found.

CHAPTER SEVEN

THE RAPID TRAMWAY

LOOKED at in terms of simple economics, the choice between trams and buses is heavily weighted in favour of the latter, which cost less to buy and, without the infrastructure needed by trams, less to run. One can understand the decision of Barrow-in-Furness, for instance, to abandon its tramways in 1932 when the cost of their renewal would have been £127,000 as against only £31,700 for new buses. Given this sort of contrast, it is surprising that other European countries did follow the example set by Britain and France in abandoning the greater part of their tramways in the thirties. The fact is, though, that decisions about public investment are rarely made simply on the basis of economics, social and political factors often being more important than the mere act of balancing the books. In prewar Germany, for example, the government encouraged the use of home-produced steel and electricity in preference to imported oil and rubber for strategic reasons, a policy which has been continued after the war in order to protect the balance of payments. And during the war itself any major changes in the belligerent countries were out of the question, and the normal market forces suspended 'for the duration'. Even after the war, although it might have made long-term economic sense to replace the shattered tramways of Germany and much of Central Europe by buses, this was quite impossible in the conditions of the time when the best that could be done was to repair existing installations as quickly as materials became available. Not that the decision to reinstate the tramways was made lightly or without an eye to the future. In Hanover, for instance, a report made shortly after the war concluded that trams should be kept on all main radial routes for reasons which included their greater carrying capacity—13,500 passengers per hour, per direction, as against 9,000 for buses—the opportunities which they offered for physically separating public from private transport, and the greater possibilities for economising on staff through the use of larger vehicles.

These three things are, in fact, the great advantages of the tram, and most postwar development has sought to capitalise on them. In the reconstruction of West German cities, for example, opportunity was taken to segregate the tram tracks from the public road wherever possible or necessary. City centre junctions were laid in large grassed islands, as in Hanover's Steintor, and high-speed tramways were built on the median strip of main roads, an excellent instance of this being along the *Ruhrschnellweg* at Essen. As well as the increased motor traffic which made such measures necessary, another fact of postwar life was a rise in the cost of wages, sometimes coupled with a shortage of labour as well. This made the old-fashioned three-car train with a crew of four uneconomic, and many countries pressed ahead with plans for the building of high-capacity bogie cars which the war had caused to be shelved. Such cars, like the Swiss standards before them, had a capacity of over 100, which was too many for the traditional roving conductor to deal with, so most of these new cars were designed on the American PAYE system, normally with a seated conductor at the rear entrance and with front and/or centre exit. This was not always the case—Bergen, for example, took delivery of 10 new centre-entrance bogies in 1947–8—but it became the norm, at least in Western Europe. In the East resources were more stretched and two-axle cars continued to be produced well into the 1960s, particularly in Eastern Germany. There labour was even scarcer than it was in the West, and three-car trains are now operated without conductors at all, usually with a woman driver, passengers having to put their money in an 'honesty box' or *zahlbox* on boarding.

In the West those countries which had already made some progress in the development of bogies were naturally first off the mark. The Swedish and Swiss examples have already been noted, and Italy resumed production of modern cars very soon after the war ended. In Milan, for instance, some war-damaged cars were rebuilt in 1947–8 and just over 50 new bogies were delivered in 1952. And in Denmark the Kobenhavns Sporveje workshops built the first of a small series of streamlined bogie

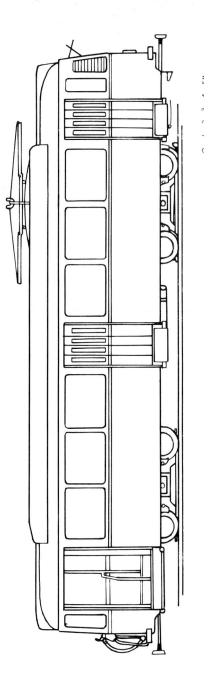

A modern single-ended bogie tram of the Basle undertaking. Its features include automatic doors, passenger-flow, high-capacity (96 passengers), air brakes and high-speed motors [*P. N. C. Cooke*]

motors in 1949, these being the first in the city to have passenger flow. Their success led to the conversion of the entire fleet of pre-war bogies and the austerity cars.

Another country which resumed the production of bogie cars at an early date was Russia. One of the first was the Leningrad type LM47, built from 1947 onwards and followed 10 years later by the LM57, an extremely handsome and successful design of which nearly 1,000 were built. Leningrad has always tended to go its own way in tramcar design, and its products certainly look more elegant than the rather pedestrian standard types which have been built for a number of Soviet cities in a factory at Riga. The prototype of the MTV-82A again dated from 1947, and like all the products of this works was a single-ended all-steel car with two sets of folding doors at front and rear. Later variations concentrated on reducing the weight of the cars until in 1956 the more powerful RVZ design was introduced. Incidentally many Soviet cities still appear to use the old-fashioned bow collector, although pantographs are gradually replacing them on the newer cars. Since the war Russia has relied heavily on imports from its satellites, first from East Germany and more recently from Czechoslovakia.

Western Germany, it will be remembered, had remained faithful to the traditional two-axle motor and trailer formation until well after the war. However by the end of the 1940s the rise in wages made the passenger-crew ratio achievable by a three-car train, 45:1, an uneconomic proposition, and Germany belatedly joined the high-capacity tramcar league. One of the first of the larger cars was the 1950 Munich type M1, which curiously enough for a city which had been using bogies since 1898, had a three-axle truck. There were only four of the original class M1, together with two matching trailers, but such was their success that similar three-axle cars became the standard Munich tram for upwards of fifteen years. The first bogie high-capacity cars—or, to use the German term, *Grossraumwagen*—appeared in Hamburg around 1950. With their sharp ends they resemble the Swiss standards as much as anything, and this, together with their red livery, makes them untypical of anything else in the Federal Republic. The archetypal German tram was in fact to appear the following year, the result of co-operation between various undertakings, notably Hanover and Düsseldorf, and the firm of Düwag. The prototype motor and trailer set was supplied to Hanover in time to enter service in April 1951, and a second, rather different pair, went to Düsseldorf in May. The Hanover cars had an all-steel body with the rounded profile and recessed windscreen which has been the trademark of most Düwag cars from that day to this. Passenger flow was incorporated, of course, with a large rear platform for passengers to wait in before passing the seated conductor. The by-now usual rubber springing and resilient wheels ensured smooth and silent running, using bogies which had been designed by the manufacturers before the war. The controller, designed by the Hanover undertaking itself, was mounted under the floor and had twenty driving notches and seventeen braking notches—a considerable improvement on traditional practice, but still nowhere near the PCC control unit. The first *Grossraumwagen* were single-ended, but double-ended versions were also built. Another variation was the use of only two motors, one to each truck, instead of the usual four, this being tried for the first time on the 1951 Düsseldorf prototype. The appearance of later models was also improved by the insertion of larger windows in place of the many small ones on the first production batches.

German undertakings seized eagerly upon the new trams, for with a capacity of about 120 they had an immediate competitive advantage over the bus. Almost all of the larger and many of the smaller systems bought them, one of the largest fleets, naturally, being that of Hanover itself where there were eventually a total of 95 motors and 93 trailers. Some of the Hanover trailers were built as non-driving motors, and ordinary motors have sometimes been used in multiple-unit pairs, as in Kiel where six such sets are operated on the one remaining route between Wellingdorf and Fähre Holtenau. Duwag found little foreign demand for its bogies, however, probably because other countries already had their own designs. Austria was about the only foreign country to buy any of them, and then only a few. The success of the high-capacity bogie car in its various national guises is, however, not in doubt, for it provided one way out of the self-defeating spiral of higher costs, higher fares and reduced patronage, the alternative being the closure of tramways in favour of the bus.

At the same time as these events were taking place in Germany, other countries were going ahead with the development of a European version of the PCC car. Of course, most modern trams embody some features of the PCC like rubber suspension and automatic control, and certain cars with sophisticated control systems, such as the later Gothenburg bogies, and even those with American-style bodies, such as some in Barcelona, have been officially described as 'variants of the PCC'. But this is rather misleading in that only those cars which use patented features stemming from the original American design can truly be described as PCCs, and it seems best to confine the designation to those which use the PCC control unit. On this definition it appears that the first European PCC was put into service as early as 1942 or 1943 in Turin, but the circumstances of the time meant that no more were built until after the war, when in 1949 Fiat resumed deliveries of PCCs to Turin. However the mainstream of development was channelled through two firms, one in Western and the other in Eastern Europe, La Brugeoise of Belgium and CKD-Tatra of Prague. To take the former first, it imported a complete American PCC for service on the SNCV, which by 1952 had a PCC fleet of 25, all except the first locally built, though still with American-style bodies. Actually PCCs did not prove particularly successful for interurban services, and these cars were sold to Belgrade in Yugoslavia in 1960. Meanwhile, however, a series of PCCs with new European-style bodies had been delivered to Brussels from 1951 onwards and had won immediate acceptance, there now being nearly 200 in service in the Belgian capital. One of them is illustrated on page 174 going down the subway ramp at the Place Ste. Catherine. The Brussels cars are rather narrow for modern vehicles at 7ft 4in (2.2m), but they still have room for 104 passengers, 32 of them seated. All equipment is worked electrically, and the car is driven by three pedals—a dead man device which brings the car to a halt automatically when released, a brake and an accelerator. Other controls are fitted on two desks in the driver's position. The cars have four motors and several alternative or complimentary systems of braking—in this case rheostatic and mechanical drum brakes, which work in concert, and magnetic track brakes for emergency use. Recent modifications have included the fitting of pantographs as well as trolley poles for use in the subways and alterations to make one-man operation possible.

The other major user of PCCs in the Low Countries in the early fifties, The Hague, preferred the American-style body, and over 70 such cars were in service by 1957 being, incidentally, one of the first large-scale fleets of one-man tramcars in Western Europe. The earliest deliveries had standee windows on the American pattern, but these were later eliminated by the use of large European picture windows, which improved the appearance of the cars considerably. In accordance with American practice none of these European PCCs haul trailers, though the cars in The Hague, at least, can run in multiple-unit. Other examples of the Belgian PCCs, this time with Brussels-style bodies, are to be found in two of the remaining French tramways at Marseilles and St Etienne and, in Belgium itself, at Antwerp and Ghent, where the ancient six-wheelers are at last being replaced. An attempt was also made to interest both Copenhagen and Hamburg, but although a test car was supplied in each case, no orders resulted.

A few other cities have used PCCs, but in most cases these have been imported secondhand from North America. Ex-Washington cars have turned up in Barcelona and Belgrade, for example, whilst Toronto has recently sold some of its older cars to Alexandria in Egypt. PCC cars, in this case locally built, were also operated in Madrid up until the end of the system in June 1972 and, right across the other side of the world, in Tokyo, where seven were built in 1955 before the uncertain future of the undertaking caused a switch to a cheaper type of tram.

Curiously enough, fewer PCCs have been built outside America in

Below   Two long trains of Tatra PCCs, with their computer-style fleet numbers, at Niedersedlitz terminus in Dresden in 1973

the West than have been built East of the Iron Curtain, the majority of them by the famous Czech firm of CKD-Tatra. It obtained a licence from the American Transit Research Corporation in 1947 and the first prototype car appeared in 1951. This was the type T1, of which about 300 were built, most of which are in service in Czech towns, particularly in Prague. Like all except the latest articulated models, these were single-ended bogies, and compared to their more modern derivatives slightly narrower at 2.4m, a feature which is accentuated by their sharply pointed ends. PCC type trucks were used, although the control gear was improved somewhat, as is natural in a car built over twenty years after the original design work was done. A very similar car has been produced by the Konstal works in Poland, and over 700 were in service in Warsaw by 1968, bringing about a considerable economy in current, staff and vehicles as a result of their higher speed and capacity as compared with the earlier type N. Problems were encountered, however, in the manufacture and maintainance of the sophisticated control gear, something which has been a common complaint amongst East European tramway undertakings encountering PCC cars for the first time.

The Polish car had already been overtaken by events before the first had been built in 1959, for the Tatra T2 had gone into production two years earlier. This differed mechanically very little from the T1, but had a new-style body which was wider with only slightly tapered ends. It was with this model that the Czech firm began its great export drive, for of the approximately 800 cars produced the majority are in service in the Soviet Union. The next development of the bogie PCC was the T3, which appeared in prototype form in 1962. The styling was improved somewhat, but the most important changes were a reduction in weight by the use of fibreglass end sections and the modification of the control equipment to include an automatic device to detect and counteract wheel slip during acceleration and braking, always a blind spot with earlier models. These design changes resulted in greatly improved performance fully comparable with private cars in city conditions. Indeed CKD-Tatra have so altered and improved the original PCC design over the years that their cars are almost a new breed, and they are perhaps better described as 'Tatras' rather than as PCCs so as to avoid any confusion with the ageing American examples of that marque. The very latest product of the Czech works is the T5, whose main external features are full-height windows and a flat roof, which give it a very modernistic appearance. All of these trams, with the exception of the earliest T1s, are designed to work in multiple-unit pairs, or even threes in the case of the Polish class 13N, to provide an extremely intensive and efficient rush-hour service.

East German systems mostly have very restricted track clearances, so when it was decided to suspend tramcar manufacture and to import Czech cars a special version of the T3 only 2.2m wide as against the normal 2.5m had to be designed. Known as the T4D these were delivered from 1968, and many are now in service in cities such as Dresden, Halle and Magdeburg. For the first time ever PCC cars have been provided with trailers for use in Germany, these being known as the type B4D. The details of these cars include three sets of folding doors, smart wrap-round windscreens, and very comfortable red and grey plastic seats on tubular frames, under which are individual and highly effective heaters. The awe-inspiring sight of two red and cream motors and a trailer storming down a reservation at speed is not easily to be forgotten! And nor is the superb acceleration, speed and ride of these cars, which makes them and their sisters among the finest tramcars in the world, if not the best of all.

One reason why the bogie PCC did not prove so popular in Western Europe as it has in the East is the recurring problem of the wage-price spiral. Even the introduction of the *Grossraumwagen* proved no more than a temporary palliative, and ways were being sought to increase the passenger-crew ratio still further. The East German solution of a long train of conductorless cars did not, at the time, seem feasible to many operators, particularly in Western Germany where the stage fare system could not easily be replaced by a flat fare, which the *zahlbox* presupposes. Hence larger cars were essential, and since the limit had been reached in terms of the rigid chassis, the obvious solution was the articulated car in which, it was thought, up to 250 passengers could be carried with only a two-man crew—an estimate which in fact turned out to be on the conservative side. The first postwar German articulated cars were produced in the mid-fifties, and had an immediate and revolutionary effect on tramways in the Federal Republic and in neighbouring countries. This seeming novelty, though, masks the fact that articulated trams can trace their lineage almost as far back as the electric car itself, if not beyond it, and that they were used in many cities long before their recent upsurge in popularity.

One of the earliest types of articulated tramcar was rather confusingly described as 'Fidler's patent steam omnibus', three of which were built by Manning, Wardle Co Ltd in 1870 for a steam tramway in Buenos Aires. A four-coupled steam locomotive formed the central compartment, to which were attached two passenger carriages each supported on a single pair of wheels. No direct link can, however, be traced between curiousities such as these and the first true articulated tram, which appeared early in the electric era in Cleveland, Ohio, to the patent of Messrs Brewer and Kriehbiel. It was built by the Kuhlmann Car Co in 1893, and consisted of two single-truck units connected by a short suspended section, the whole being a very handsome and well-appointed vehicle. Amongst the claims made for it were that it was safer than an ordinary motor and trailer, as well as being more economical in staff and in electrical equipment than two single units would have been. It is not known how many, and indeed whether more of these cars were built, for the idea, though a good one, was really before its time. Street railway managements were riding the crest of a wave of prosperity, and were simply not interested in penny-pinching economies, particularly as wages were low at the time. A similar experiment which took place in Milan in 1904–5, involving the connection of two cars by a short trailer with a passageway between all three, did not even have the virtue of working properly, and was again far in advance of any real need for such an arrangement. It was not until labour and material costs began to rise sharply just before World War I, and then only in America, that operators began to reconsider the idea.

The methods of joining body sections are legion, but the two which have been used in North America are the flexible diaphragm or bellows, already familiar from railway corridor connections, and the circular pivotted section known as a drum. All the early American cars used the former in connection with a suspended centre section which formed a bridge between the two car bodies. In 1913 the Virginia Railway and Power Co of Richmond put into service the first of a series of ten cars built on this pattern, in this case with normal rear entrances and with eight seats in the suspended section, the whole equipage being christened 'two rooms and a bath', a name which has stuck to this kind of arrangement ever since. In the same year Boston put a similar unit on the road, again, like the Richmond ones, made up from two older four-wheel cars, although in this case the entrance was in the centre section, as it had been on the original Cleveland car. The economy in staff, together with the new lease of life afforded to their out-dated rolling stock, so attracted the management of the Boston Elevated that it built a total of 69 similar units within the next two years, followed by 122 larger ones made up from old bogie cars, the last of which appeared in 1919. These were, however, no more than a stopgap until a new fleet of centre-entrance bogies, based on experience gained with the articulated cars, was delivered in the 1920s, and the last of the rebuilds was withdrawn in 1925. The only other American cities to use articulated cars other than experimentally were Baltimore, Cleveland and Milwaukee, the majority of them being found in the latter city where they formed a high proportion of the fleet during the interwar years. Most of these post-World War I cars were still rebuilds, but the old 'two-rooms' design was replaced by a neater single-articulation, usually of the drum type, except in Milwaukee, resting on a central bogie. Quite a few 'one-off' designs were produced experimentally, but were rejected for one reason or another by the cities concerned. The most remarkable of these was a three-section, four-bogie car built for Detroit in 1924. Although similar cars have been built in Europe more recently, this remained unique for many years as it was really too large for street running. The seating capacity was 140, and as there was room for a large number of standing passengers as well, three conductors were needed to deal with them, which rather nullified any possible economies. The great exception to the practice of splicing together articulated cars from pairs of old ones was the 188 two-section three-bogie cars built for the interurban Key System in California between 1937 and 1938, some of them using salvaged parts from other cars, but all being virtually new when completed. They could run in trains of up to five cars, and although most of the route was on private right-of-way, some of it was street running which must have caused awesome traffic jams! When the cars were withdrawn in 1958 they were sold to the General Urquiza rapid transit line in Buenos Aires. These were the last articulated cars to be built for a street tramway in the United States, for the famous Electroliners of the Chicago and North Shore interurban were intended only for private right-of-way operation.

Viewed in the light of present events it would be easy to exaggerate the importance of the articulated car in America. But in fact there were never more than a few hundred of them, mostly rebuilds, amongst the tens of thousands of ordinary streetcars, and they were used on only twelve or thirteen systems, and then only experimentally on five of these. In most of Europe during the same period articulated cars were, if possible, even less popular than in the United States. In fact, discounting the Milan experiment, the first European version did not appear until 1923 and most of those which followed it were either 'one-off' proto-types or the familiar 'two-rooms-and-a-bath' rebuilds. The main reason for European lack of interest in the idea was that pressure of costs, par-ticularly wages, was much less than it was in America.

A few experimental designs were produced in Germany from 1925, when two single-articulated three-bogie cars were built for Duisburg by a shipyard during a slump. Two cars were also built for Dresden, which later bought a solitary example from Leipzig, and two more for Berlin. The latter, dating from 1930, were four-axle cars on the 'two-rooms' pattern, Germany's first. In addition Munich, Mannheim and Frankfurt experimented with pairs of old cars connected by a simple diaphram, but these were not true articulated cars. In the case of Frankfurt two exper-iments were made, the first involving two motors and the other a motor and trailer, both units being christened 'Max und Moritz Wagen'. The former set embodied several improvements such as pass-enger-flow and transverse tubular steel seats, but like most non-standard arrangements failed to mix satisfactorily with normal trams. The second unit was used for a number of years on a city sightseeing service. A presentday example of this kind of construction is Dresden works car 721–022–4—the complicated numbers are for a comput-er—made up from two old clerestory-roofed passenger cars. Yet a third experiment in Frankfurt involved the permanent coupling of a motor and trailer between which was a passageway for the use of the conductor alone, so saving one conductor, though, one imagines, at the expense of overworking the other! In some other cases two-axle motors have been permanently coupled back-to-back to avoid reversals at termini, though not necessarily with any connection between the two cars. The only other actual articulated car built in Germany before the war was intended by the two firms concerned as a demonstration model, and was never used in public service. This had a double-articulated body supported on an unique set of four single-axle trucks, two under the centre sections and one under each end. Just about the only other articulated trams to be built new before the war were a series of 10 three-bogie cars ordered by the Dutch NZHM in the early thirties. These heavy interurbans, which were used on the line between The Hague and Leiden, were single-ended and could haul a trailer when required. Successful though they were, however, they were not imitated at the time for the reasons already stated.

In fact the only European country to make any extensive use of articulation in the two decades after 1930 was Italy. Here of course bogies were already popular, and the problem arose of what to do with the large fleets of older two-axle cars which, in comparison with the bogies, were uneconomic. A policy of wholesale scrapping was obviously out of the question, so many undertakings rebuilt them into articulated cars of various patterns. The process was begun before 1939 with, for example, the Milan class 3000 of 1932, and continued at an accelerated rate during and after the war. 'Two-rooms-and-a-bath' cars included Milan's 4000 class, reconstructed from some of its oldest two-axle cars in 1942, and about 70, which are still in use, built between 1951 and 1959 for Turin, some of the original cars in this case being bogies. Genoa also had 15 cars of this type constructed from 1920s stock in 1954–5, but these were uncommon in consisting of two motors instead of the more usual motor-trailer formation so they could be used without turning circles. Most of the early American cars were of this reversible pattern too, incidentally. An alternative design, also found in Genoa, was a single-articulated car made up from an old two-axle motor and trailer, but with the trailer truck replaced by a bogie. Other early postwar examples of articulated cars were to be found in Calcutta and Algiers, where they were needed to cope with very heavy loadings. The Calcutta cars are still in service, but the Algiers system closed in the 1950s. By this time German undertakings had at last begun to appreciate the advantages of articulation, and rebuilds were produced from 1953 based on postwar KSW or *Verbandstyp* cars. Four-axle units with suspended centre-sections were produced in places such as Duisburg and Dortmund, and one or two undertakings such as Kassel and Dortmund acquired new cars built on the same pattern. In Hamburg new, or perhaps more strictly *Aufbau*, cars were built on trucks from scrapped vehicles. In other cases the Genoa design using a single-articulation and a bogie under the rear half was preferred as, for instance, in Aachen, whilst Bremen built over 50 cars with one rigid truck and one trailing axle. In all cases, though, despite the increased capacity, all the disadvantages of the old two-axle truck were perpetuated in the form of noise, bad riding and slow speed. A really modern articulated car obviously needed to be designed from first principles rather than simply being the result of patching up old cars.

As a matter of fact the three-bogie two-section car had already been around for a long time, and a really modern version had been built many years before, only no-one had taken much notice outside its country of origin—which, not surprisingly, was Italy. The car concerned was built in 1939 for one of the two tramway systems in Rome and embodied an improved form of articulation designed by an engineer named Urbinati. This was a ring type support rather like a turntable instead of the pivots over each axle of a bogie which had been used previously. Another improvement which was owed to Italy was the substitution of telescopic panels for the old bellows connections between car sections, which had given articulated cars a rather makeshift look. Some of the other modern articulated cars produced in Italy were the 1100 class in Genoa and the 4500 class in Milan, both of which were streamlined double-ended cars modelled on contemporary bogie cars. These were built in 1942 and wartime conditions meant that both classes were small, and most Italian articulated cars have thereafter had to be rebuilds. The latest of these are some massive four-bogie three-section cars built by Milan from some older bogie cars with a total capacity of 332. It should be noted that the very high capacity achieved by European trams is a result of having far less seats than is normal on a British bus—these Milan cars, for example, have only fifty-seven seats, which means there are 275 standing passengers, the principle being that it is better to stand on the vehicle than at the stop.

The first really modern articulated tram in Western Germany was built in 1953 for Stuttgart using the six-axle design with a central bogie known, incidentally, as a Jacobs bogie. Only five of these cars were ever built, however, and it took five years to do it, so the real breakthrough did not come until later, in 1956, when Düwag introduced its version of the six-axle car with a newly-designed articulation in Bochum and Dusseldorf. With a capacity of 200 it proved an immediate success and orders came flooding in, with about twenty systems deciding to introduce articulated cars. The economic situation had, in fact, been entirely changed, for even the largest bus with a two-man crew could only offer a passenger-crew ratio of 75:1, whereas the new trams had a ratio of 100:1. Some systems, of course, had such a volume of traffic that they would not have considered abandoning the trams even without the possibility of using articulated cars, but other smaller systems would undoubtedly have succumbed without them.

Meanwhile the staff situation was getting even worse, for not only were wages rising, but there was a serious staff shortage. One way of dealing with this was to produce an even bigger articulated car, and Düwag did this almost immediately in 1957 when the prototype eight-axle car was delivered to Düsseldorf. This was really a six-axle car with an additional centre section and, of course, an extra bogie under the second articulation. These cars had a capacity of about 250, which meant that the passenger-crew ratio had been improved still further. Those undertakings which had invested heavily in *Grossraumwagen* were rather ·stuck by these new developments. Some of them, like Hanover, virtually ignored the articulated car, but others had their bogie cars rebuilt into six or eight-axle units; and later on some of the original six-axle cars had new centre sections added to bring them up to the latest standards. There is, of course, a vast variety of articulated car in Western Germany, not just the Düwag types already mentioned. Some have three-axle trucks, like some rather unsuccessful ones built for Munich; others, notably the famous Esslingen GT4 cars, have only two bogies, one at each end, the articulation being supported by a sub-frame; one of the latest, at Duisburg, has as many as ten axles.

This is, however, running ahead rather. Once the success of the Düwag cars had been proved in Germany other countries began to show interest in the economies offered by articulation, one of the first being Holland, where six-axle cars were introduced in both Amsterdam and Rotterdam in 1957. Both types were of a very distinctive design, and owed a lot to Swiss influence. The bodies of the Amsterdam cars were built by a Dutch firm under Swiss licence, their most obvious 'local' feature being an extremely large destination indicator with room for the

Above Six-axle Düwag articulated car, with a modern half-pantograph and the typical recessed windscreen, towing a Swiss-built trailer in Basle [*Basler Verkehrsbetriebe*

colour code still used on Amsterdam trams. The Rotterdam cars were part of an order which also included 15 bogies, and both types were modelled on the Basle lightweight bogies of 1952 with the same non-motored rear truck and downward sloping floor, which meant that the first two bogies on the articulated car were motored instead of the more usual front and rear. The articulations were of the Urbinati type. Obviously the lightweight design must have been more successful in Rotterdam than it was in Basle, although later on the city ordered some ordinary Düwag cars. Düwag, in fact, was able to build up quite a large export order book with, for example, 100 cars going to Copenhagen between 1960 and 1968, and others to Basle, together with some built under licence by Austrian firms for use in Vienna and Graz. Vienna, incidentally, has perpetuated both of the older forms of articulated tram as well with its type D, a 'two-rooms' design built from two old trailers, and the type F, a completely new version of the four-axle truck with trailing bogie.

Other countries where bogie trams were already well-established were not always as quick to follow suit. Belgian tramways, for instance, still rely almost exclusively on bogies, although La Brugeoise is now building an articulated version of its PCC car, most of them for Brussels. The major Swiss tramways too were rather slow off the mark, with Zurich taking delivery of its first, and only, six-axle single-articulated

car as late as 1960. In 1962, however, both Basle and Zurich experimented with a completely new design of six-axle double-articulated
tram, which dispensed with the usual Jacobs bogie underneath each articulation, replacing them by a single bogie in the centre of the middle section between the two joints. Zurich has taken most readily to these new
cars, and now operates many of its routes with multiple-unit trains of
two such cars together.

The Communist block in general is only now beginning to build articulated cars on any scale as the widespread use of unstaffed trailers removed one of the main justifications for their very high initial cost.
However, single units do have other advantages, including the obviation
of shunting operations, which take both time and manpower, and also
the reduction in weight as compared to capacity, which leads to economy in current consumption and improved performance. For instance a
Hanover bogie motor weighs 16.9 tonnes, whereas a six-axle articulated
car is only 3.1 tonnes heavier, far less than a motor-trailer unit. So now
most East European manufacturers have produced their own versions of
the articulated car, the most notable being the Tatra T4, a six-axle derivative of the famous bogie PCCs, and those built by the Hungarian firm
of Ganz. The latter were developed especially for Budapest, and the cars
used there are double-ended eight-axle units with the minimum of seating and a total capacity of 272. So when used in multiple-unit, and without a conductor in the front car, 544 passengers can be carried with a
crew of only two. The cars have chassis-mounted motors connected to
the bogies via long propeller shafts and couplings. The external styling
is rather more angular than usual, with a square end and flat roof, giving
a very pleasing appearance. Also worthy of note are the various articulated cars produced by the Konstal works in Poland, and other eastern
bloc countries, such as Russia and Rumania, are now building their own
articulated trams, and most cars built in the future are likely to be of this
pattern.

Outside Europe articulated cars have only been used in the places
mentioned and in Japan, where a number of quite modern units has been
put into service in recent years. These include about 50 delivered in the
mid-sixties to Sapporo in the north of the country, the later series being a
particularly handsome design with very deep windows and the unique,
for Japan, arrangement of a seated conductor and passenger flow. Both

sections of these cars are numbered separately, as A801/802, which is the same system as was used on the Dutch NZHM interurban. Sapporo has also linked pairs of modern bogies by a bellows connection, recalling the similar, though less successful experiments carried out in prewar Germany. True articulated cars are also to be found in other places, such as Kitakyushu, on the southern island of Kyushu, but in general Japan's tramways are in decline, and most of the remaining ones still rely primarily on bogies.

It will be evident that most of the larger tramway systems of the world now rely almost exclusively on modern high-capacity bogie cars, often PCCs, and on articulated trams, which are increasingly becoming the norm. There are exceptions, Vienna still has a large number of two-axle cars, as do East German undertakings; and in some other places, such as Melbourne and Toronto, a new generation of bogie cars is being planned. But just about the only areas where articulated cars are not to be found at all are Australasia, Scandinavia, now that the Copenhagen cars have been sold to Alexandria, and North America, where it all began 50 years ago. This anomaly is, however, likely to be put right in the near future, for Boston, Philadelphia and San Francisco are going to replace their PCCs with new articulated cars by the mid-seventies.

The articulated tramcar must now have reached about the ultimate in size, at least as far as street running tramways are concerned, and no further economies can be expected in this direction. Costs continue to rise, and a tramway system must either go into deficit or find new ways of paring costs, particularly wages, unless it raises fares to an unacceptable level. The maximum number of passengers any conductor can be expected to deal with is about 250, which would seem to make the eight-axle tramcar the largest possible unit. As a matter of fact far larger trams are already in service, and the explanation of this apparent paradox is the replacement of traditional fare structures by new ones which have made it possible to dispense with the conductor altogether. One-man trams are not new, of course—they were common enough in horse-car days, and many electric tramways have used them since. The American PCC was built to be operated by one man, and this was done in The Hague when PCCs were introduced there, whilst other smaller European systems have operated two-axle cars without conductors. The Scandinavian towns of Halsingborg and Aarhus have, for instance, used the American 'pay-as-you-leave' system, passengers having to pay the driver or, in the case of trailers in Aarhus, the conductor, on exit. Change machines were provided on the Aarhus trams so that the exact fare could be tendered. More recently Brussels has used its rebuilt 9000 class as one-man cars, and the PCCs can now be operated by one man also. The difference, though, between these examples and the situation today is that the modern articulated tram can carry so many more people even than a PCC—far more than the driver could issue tickets for without excessive delays.

A first step towards the elimination of conductors, which was taken in both parts of Germany, was to withdraw the conductor from one trailer which was then available only to season ticketholders. West German systems now often attach a bogie or a two-axle trailer to an articulated car for this purpose. The logical progression from this is, of course, the East German *zahlbox*, but this has a number of deficiencies. The main one in the past was that it could not cope with a stage fare structure, although this is a less cogent objection now that fares have been simplified in many cases. As it happens the *zahlbox* is occasionally used for stage fares, but only for small systems like the Woltersdorfer Strassenbahnen near Berlin, which has only one short line and two stages. Interestingly enough certain East German systems are now replacing their honesty boxes with the system to be described below, possibly because fare evasion is becoming more of a problem. Another problem though is that transfers are impossible, and this would rule out the fare box system in most West European cities.

Hence the solution that has been adopted in many places is the issue of tickets before the journey commences and their validation at the time of travel and, where appropriate, when any change of vehicle is made. Tickets are sold from the numerous kiosks which are found in continental cities, from offices of the transport undertaking, or from machines, or from any combination of these. Usually pre-purchased tickets are sold in bulk and at a reduced rate to encourage their use, so imposing a penalty on cash customers, where these are allowed at all. To reduce the load on the system frequent use is made of all-day 'ride-at-will' tickets or of season tickets, valid either for a whole tramway system or for one or more particular routes. The variety of such fare systems is tremendous, but the key to them all is the automatic canceller, or validator as the Europeans prefer to call it. Two systems can be described.

In Kiel tickets may be purchased at a flat rate either from machines at the principal stops or from the driver (without any financial penalty). Each ticket entitles the holder to an initial journey and to two changes, probably subject to a time limit. Passengers using their tickets for the first or second time may enter the cars by any door except the front half of the driver's door—passenger-flow ceases to have any raison d'etre under this system—and cancel their tickets in an *entwerter* on the grab rail. Only passengers making a second change and those wanting to buy a ticket need pass the driver, so making it easier for him to cope with all the duties required. Since there are no conductors at all, not even on the trailers, there is no-one to open the doors, so a self-service button is provided at each door except the driver's clearly indicated by a notice and a red arrow. In this way Kiel operates multiple-unit trains of two *Grossraumwagen* and six-axle articulated cars plus a two-axle trailer with only one man apiece, giving in the latter case a passenger-crew ratio of 250:1, far superior to the one-man articulated bus at 154:1.

An alternative to this system is that used in Zurich, where a combined ticket-issueing and cancelling machine is provided at every stop, and there are none on the tram. One reason for this is that Zurich has less stops than it has vehicles! Also it is necessary for the point of origin to be indicated on the cancellation, as a cheaper ticket is available for up to five stops, and a tramborne machine could not do this. Hence passengers either buy a ticket of the appropriate value from the machine, which issues it ready cancelled, or they cancel part of a multi-ride ticket in another slot, and then board the tram without further formality. Düsseldorf uses cancellers on which the time and stage *number* can be altered by the driver, but it is not possible to show the stage in an abbreviated spelt out form, as is the case in Zurich. Bogie motor-trailer sets and multiple-unit pairs of articulated trams are operated in Zurich, all with only a driver, which has meant that platform staff could be more than halved, without either reducing services or raising fares, which would otherwise have been inevitable.

Most of this chapter has so far been concerned with the possibilities for economy offered by large-sized tramcars and, by implication, with their greater carrying capacity as opposed to the bus. Very little has been said about the equally important question of the segregation of public from private transport, where the tram has a great advantage over its nearest rival. Of course, it is perfectly possible to build private roads for buses, analogous to tramway reservations, and some cities, like Pittsburgh, have or will be doing this. But when it comes to more sophisticated forms of segregation, like viaducts or subways, the bus is at a severe disadvantage—in both cases because it needs more space than a guided vehicle like a tram, and in the latter because of the problem of air pollution. Also its capacity is less, which means that expensive installations are used at less than their optimum efficiency. The tram is, in fact, the most flexible of all public transport vehicles, for it can go virtually anywhere, above, below, beside or in the street.

Tramway reservations date back to before World War I, or even earlier in the case of interurbans. One of the most successful lines built on this pattern is the Shaker Heights Rapid Transit in Cleveland, Ohio, which is entirely on reservation, much of it without any road crossings at all. Most of the system, which consists of a main line and two branches, dates from 1920, although it was not until 1930 that the last part into central Cleveland was taken off the street and onto the railway tracks which it now shares with a heavy rapid transit line. Large car parks at many of the stations encourage people to leave their cars to ride into the centre on the trains of PCC streetcars, of which Shaker Heights has a total of 55. Many more miles of urban tramways have been placed on reservations since World War II, one of the most remarkable instances of this being Gothenburg, where a very ordinary street-running tramway system has been extended and realigned so that today the major part of the nine tram routes is on reservation, except in the city centre. One of the most interesting extensions was that to Frölundatorg, opened in 1963 along tracks shared for some distance with a diesel railway, and more recently new rapid tramways have been opened to Hjällbo (1969) and Bergsjön (1970). In Zurich part of one of the main shopping streets, Bahnhofstrasse, has been made into a pedestrian tram precinct with the trams continuing to run through, free from other traffic and only having pedestrians to contend with.

But such schemes have not proved adequate to keep service speeds up in the face of congestion caused by the private car, mainly because it is only in rare cases that reservations can be provided in the city centre, which is where they are most needed. One of these rare cases is Dresden, where until recently there was still a considerable amount of war damage to be cleared up, meaning that opportunity could be taken to provide long sections of completely segregated track right in the centre of the city. Particularly impressive is the new Dr Rudolphs Friedrichs Brücke, which has two lanes for motor traffic and double tram tracks to one side of these. However in most cases some sort of second level where trams could operate unimpeded was felt to be necessary. There have been proposals for tramways on viaducts, and some such lines have been built, particularly in the Netherlands, but the preferred solution has usually been the tram subway, and this has perhaps been the most significant development of recent years.

Just as with articulated cars, though, it has not exactly been a recent innovation. Before going any further it would be as well to define the terms as used here. A tunnel is taken as being an underground diversion made necessary by a natural obstacle, as on a railway, and it may or may not have stations within it, but usually does not. A subway, on the other hand, is an underground section of tramway made necessary by traffic congestion, and it usually does have stations. Of course, a tunnel may incidentally relieve traffic congestion, but this is not its main purpose. Examples of now-closed tramway tunnels include those in Wellington, New Zealand, in Genoa, 'in which', Baedeker warned his readers at the turn of the century, 'the temperature is low', and in Yokohama. Still in use are the Twin Peaks and the Sunset Tunnels in San Francisco, opened respectively in 1918 and 1920, the former with two stations within its length of 11,920ft. Much more recently a short length of tunnel, including a station has been built on a new extension in Gothenburg, but generally tramways have preferred to avoid obstacles rather than to undertake expensive public works which are really more appropriate to a railway.

In Budapest Europe's first underground electric railway, dating from 1896, still operates in almost its original form. But although it has many tramway characteristics, such as overhead current collection and the use of only one or two-car trains, it is not really a tramway subway as no through services are operated with the surface lines. At about the same time, however, traffic congestion was bringing Boston's streetcars almost to a halt in peak hours, and to alleviate this the Tremont Street subway, the world's first, was opened in two stages in 1897 and 1898.

The number of cars using Tremont Street rose from 200 to 400 per hour each way, and in its first year of operation the subway was used by 50 million passengers. After that three more tram subways were built, the first, the East Boston, later being converted to heavy rapid transit. The others, along Boylston Street and Huntingdon Avenue, run into the original subway and are still in use as part of Boston's Green Line, as the streetcar system is known. All of the remaining routes feed into the subways, including a new extension to Riverside opened in 1959 along the course of an old railway line. Modernisation plans are now well in hand, and include the purchase of new cars, track improvements and new maintenance facilities, which will ensure the place of the streetcar in Boston's transit system for the foreseeable future.

Other early examples of subways in the United States are to be found in Newark, where a five-mile line was constructed on the bed of a disused canal in the 1930s, and in Philadelphia, where part of the Market Street Subway was opened in 1905, with a new extension as recently as 1955. Traffic problems were not so bad in other countries, so major subway systems on the American pattern were correspondingly rarer. In Britain there was the famous Kingsway Subway, opened by the LCC for single-deck cars between 1906 and 1908, and rebuilt for double-deckers in 1930–31. The subway routes were the last to run north of the Thames and were withdrawn shortly before the closure of the whole system in 1952. Another former tramway subway still exists in Stockholm, but this has now been incorporated into a conventional underground railway. In Marseilles, though, a single tram route has survived because its terminal station is in a short length of subway, actually dating from 1893, when it was opened as a steam light railway, but not electrified until 1905.

It was after World War II, though, when traffic congestion on the American scale became more of a reality in Europe, that the tram subway really came into its own. The most significant developments have taken place in Western Germany, where between 10 and 15 cities have built or are building sections of tram subway, though one of the earliest and to date most comprehensive developments has taken place in Brussels. It might be as well here to say something about the differences between an underground tramway and an underground railway, although as we shall see these differences are tending to become very blurred. However, a tramway as opposed to a railway does not have to be signalled but, assuming that the tunnels are lit, can be operated on sight as it is on the surface; it usually uses trains of at most three cars instead of longer ones; it usually loads from pavement level rather than from a high platform; there are often more junctions in a tram subway than there would be in a railway one; and, of course, the tramway can return to the street or reservation after leaving the subway, whereas a railway is normally completely segregated. These differences mean that a tramway subway is cheaper to build than a full-scale underground railway, and also that it can be built in stages as required. That means, for instance, that if there is a particularly congested junction it can be put underground fairly quickly and the tramway led up to the surface again by temporary ramps which can be removed once the tunnel is extended, if that is the intention. Had it been a railway, the whole lot would have had to be built at one go, instead of in stages. This is what is happening in most cities where tram subways are being built, which probably explains why most of them are at the *hauptbahnhof* since this is the focus of public transport in most German cities. Subways are built in one of two ways, either by tunnelling or by digging up the street and then filling it in again, a method usually known as 'cut and cover'. Both are extremely expensive, and the process can take a very long time, five years or more, so cities only undertake this sort of investment when they are very sure that it is needed.

The first subway in Brussels was built as early as 1958, when, as part of the improvements made necessary by the international exposition of that year, the busy junction at the Gare du Midi was put underground. Two much longer subways are now open, meaning that most of the city centre is now completely free of surface tramways. The second of these follows one of the outer boulevards round the city centre, but the first, which was opened in the winter of 1969–70, has a completely new route right across, or rather under, the old part of the town. It starts at a surface station in the Place Ste Catherine, and then the ramp immediately disappears under a church! There are six stations on this particular section, and the tunnel itself consists of a concrete-lined tube. There are some quite steep gradients on the line, and one sharp bend between the Parc and Arts/Kunst stations. At the end of the subway two ramps give access to the ordinary tram tracks, which on three of the subway routes are almost entirely on reservation, which makes a very fast and efficient service possible. Few other towns have made as much progress as Brussels, and some have no more than a couple of underground junctions or a short central subway, which in some cases, as for instance in Kassel, is as much as is intended. The three West German systems which have made most progress, though in rather different ways, are Cologne, Frankfurt and Stuttgart. The last was the first to go in for subways in a big way, and the initial section was opened as early as 1966. Lengthy additions have been made since that time, and now underground routes cross the city centre in both directions. Allied to this has been a policy of extending tram routes into the suburbs, something which has been happening in many other West German cities such as Cologne and Munich. The former's first subway was opened in 1968, first of all with a stub terminus at Dom/Hauptbahnhof, and later on as a through route with several ramps connected to the surface lines. Frankfurt's system is rather different, for it partakes much more of the character of an underground railway. For a start stations both in the subway and on the surface sections have high platforms and most of the paraphanalia one associates with railway stations. Some new and very handsome six-axle articulated cars have been purchased for the new lines, and these too look rather more like railway trains than trams. Except, of course, that railway carriages are not usually articulated, and nor do they have steps, which these need in order to operate in the street, which this class, designated U2, is expected to do. To make matters more confusing, ordinary tramcars also run in the subway, and in order to allow *them* to stop at the station platforms they have been slightly widened on one side and special folding steps fitted. The first route, opened in 1968, runs via a 4km tunnel and then via normal central reservation—except that it is fenced off almost throughout—from the town centre to a new suburb called Nordweststadt, where there is another short length of tunnel. Other routes have now been brought into the system, generally running in a north-south direction across the city centre. A new class of tramcar has also been produced, and these are eight-axle articulated cars a little narrower than the earlier U2s.

Subways are being built or are in use in a number of other West German towns, particularly those in the Ruhr, where Essen has made the most progress, and in Hanover. The latter has had a subway station completed for a number of years, but contrary to usual practice does not intend to use it until the whole of the first underground line is completed. Special rolling stock has been designed here too, and the eventual plan is for four cross-city underground routes. Subways are not confined to the Federal Republic, of course—Vienna has built a number of underground tramways, for instance—but it is true to say that the concept has found most favour there. Nor are subways the only way of dealing with city-centre congestion. In The Hague, for example, tramways are being placed on viaducts in the central area, mainly because some roads are being put underground, which would mean that tramways would have to be put much deeper than normal to avoid them. Other examples of elevated tramways are to be found in Nurnberg and Rotterdam. Another approach which has been tried is traffic restraint. One of the first towns to do this was Bremen, where only public transport is allowed into the old heart of the city. Gothenburg has recently imitated this, although traffic has not been banned completely, but simply confined to certain zones from which it is not permitted to cross to another, so ensuring clear runs for trams passing through the area as a whole. This experiment has only been a qualified success, for all that has been done is to transfer the hold-ups further out of the centre. Probably subways or something like them will have to be built in the end, but traffic restraint can be a useful palliative, and indeed will probably have to come to most of our cities in time.

This is the new tramway then—segregated, articulated, automated. But time does not stand still, and one cannot expect the tramway ever again to give the impression that it does. So whither the tram in the year 2000?

CHAPTER EIGHT

THEN?... AND THEN

EUROPEAN TRAMWAYS have already changed almost beyond recognition from their condition before and immediately after World War II and have become what is really a different transport mode—light rapid transit as opposed to the old-fashioned street tramway. The trends towards the improvement of rolling stock, the mechanisation of fare collection and the segregation of the track are likely to continue, and this carries with it certain implications for the future. On the one hand those smaller systems which have not already closed are unlikely to survive for very long because of the prohibitive costs of modernising a tramway in this way. There are, of course, exceptions to this rule. Neunkirchen, for instance, has retained a single tramway route because of a very steep hill which buses cannot negotiate in winter, whilst St Etienne uses trams because of the very heavy loadings experienced on its one line. And Eastern European countries have generally tended to use trams in circumstances in which they would have long disappeared in the west, but even here as tramways are modernised and private motoring increases, the smaller systems are beginning to be abandoned. The other consequence of this continued process of modernisation is that even those large systems which are retained may not be very easily recognisable as tramways in a few decades time. Of course, someone writing of today from the standpoint of the 1930s could say the same thing, but it is in fact the stated intention of many of these larger undertakings to convert their systems to something much more akin to an underground or urban railway than to a tramway as we know it today.

This trend can already be seen from the fact that very few of the existing underground tramways are so described—but instead such phrases as semi-metro, pre-metro or even underground railway are used. This nomenclature may conceal various intentions. On the one hand it may simply be an unwillingness to use the rather unfashionable word 'tramway' in connection with a new development. Hence Cologne's subways are described as a *U-bahn*, even though they are and are intended to remain tram subways pure and simple. On the other hand the use of a different term may be an attempt to indicate that the modernised tramway is indeed a new transport mode, as in The Hague where the term semi-metro is used to show that their new transit system is something mid-way between a traditional tramway and a full-scale urban railway. More often, though, the use of 'railway' terminology indicates the intention to up-grade the tramways to railway standards in the forseeable future. So when Brussels describes its lines as a pre-metro it means that they are to be converted at a later stage to a full metro, and the same implication lies behind the German phrases like *U-bahn* and *Stadtbahn*.

The reason why many cities intend to up-grade their tramways in this way is not any prejudice against the tram, but simply that, even on segregated track, it is not capable of coping with the traffic flows envisaged by the end of this century. The Hanover undertaking has calculated that an underground tramway can take 16,000 passengers per hour per direction, and although this is perhaps a conservative estimate, it is nowhere near the 30,000 which an underground railway can take. This difference is accounted for by such factors as the longer trains and better signalling of a railway as opposed to a tramway, and also by the use of high platforms which speed up loading and hence reduce the time spent at stations. So most of the subways which have been constructed are designed for eventual up grading, being built to take wider and longer trains than at present use them. Various temporary arrangements have been made to accommodate the trams which now operate the services. Frankfurt already uses high platforms together with the dual-level steps already described. In Brussels the stations have high platforms, but a bay has been cut down to pavement level to accommodate the trams in the interim before full metro operation. Stuttgart, where conversion to a full-scale *U-bahn* is some way in the future, has pavement level platforms throughout. Another large scheme, perhaps the most ambitious of them all, involves the Ruhr area where several tramway systems already work

Above A Brussels PCC bogie disappears into the tunnel at the start of the cross-city subway in the Place Ste Catherine

closely together. These tramways are mostly metre-gauge, and the plan calls for their eventual replacement by a standard gauge interurban railway system known as a *Stadtbahn*.

The adoption of an urban railway of whatever type does not necessarily mean that tramways will be eliminated entirely. *U-bahn, Stadtbahn* and tramway co-exist quite happily in East Berlin, for example, just as the underground, the main line railways and the tramways used to do in London. And even where some tram routes are up-graded or replaced, others may be retained or even extended despite the building of a metro. This is already happening in Rotterdam, for example, where most of the existing system is being retained and new extensions are being made even though a metro has been opened as well. A new express tram route was opened in 1968 to act as a feeder to the metro, and in the following year a completely new route was inaugurated to serve the suburb of

Schiebroek. All of it is on reservation, and it includes an 860m long viaduct over a canal, a railway and a road, providing an uninterupted run into central Rotterdam. Munich is another city which has decided to dispense with the intermediate stage of a tram subway and to go straight ahead with a full-scale *U-bahn*. But this has not meant a cessation of the programme of tramway extensions into the outer suburbs, and trams will continue to have an important place in the city's transport. In Brussels, too, even when the tunnel routes are converted into full metros, many tram lines will remain, either as segregated rapid tramways or as ordinary street tramways. Similar developments are taking place in Eastern Europe, though the tram subway as such has found less favour there, probably because at least in the past traffic congestion was less severe.

Two cities where this process of up-grading and replacement of tramways has already been completed are Stockholm and Oslo. In the Swedish capital parts of the tram routes, including the tram subway mentioned earlier, have been incorporated into the *T-bana* system, which now provides the greater part of the city's transport, and only one tram route has been retained as a feeder. Oslo provides a most interesting

Below The latest type of eight-axle articulated tram in Frankfurt has special folding steps designed to cope with both street and platform loading   [*Stadtwerke Frankfurt-am-Main*

case, which has received less attention than it has deserved, of the changeover from a tramway to a railway. The city has always presented a confusing picture to the transport enthusiast who thought he could distinguish a tram from a train, with two suburban tramways, ordinary city tramways, and a group of lines operated by single vehicles with conductors, which might be trams too if they did not start in a tunnel and have high platform stations and more-or-less segregated track. One of the suburban tramways, which must incidentally have had one of the longest names ever accorded to a tram route, the LilleakerØstenjobbanen, ran across the city from west to east. Its western terminus was and is at Jar, a station shared with the high-platform Kolsåsbanen, so the LOB cars are provided with a special pavement-level section. This part of the route, as far as the town centre, is still operated by the unique prewar *Guldfiskar* or 'fish-tail' bogie trams. The eastern section of route was up-graded during the 1950s as part of a planned underground railway. A branch, known as the Lambertseterbanen, was opened in 1957 and an extension of the original route from Oppsal to Boler in 1958. All of this was still operated by tram—the LOB and city route 3 to Boler and route 4 along the branch. At the same time a tunnel for the underground railway was being built in the city centre, but this was never, on the by-now usual pattern, used by trams. Instead the trams running on the surface routes were replaced in stages in 1966–7, and the railway system now totals four branches. It had originally been intended to link the underground section with the older western lines, but this is now unlikely, and future investment will be put into other completely new routes. Trams still run on four city routes, together with the suburban lines to Jar and Ljabru.

To prophesy is dangerous, but it seems more than likely that the tramcar, as we know it today, will have a useful role to play in city transport for many years to come. In the larger cities its role may well be a subsidiary rather than a dominant one, but in smaller and medium-sized places a modern tramway is well able to cope with all the demands likely to be made upon a local transport system. Moreover the energy crisis which developed late in 1973, and the inevitable decline of oil as a source of power, may well place the tram in an even stronger position, for most of the new sources of energy, such as nuclear or solar power, are directed towards the production of electricity. Also railed transport of any kind is a much more efficient user of energy than road vehicles, which cannot but be taken into account in a time of energy shortage. A pointer to the way things are going is the recent decision to convert and extend some British Rail lines in Newcastle to form a new rapid transit system which, apart from the lack of street-running sections, will be somewhat akin to the Frankfurt U-bahn.

That the tram has a future is certain, but, except for museums, its past is disappearing. Only a few years ago most European systems presented the spectacle of 50-year old cars running in concert with the latest products from Düwag or wherever, but now closures and modernisation—often accelerated by legislation such as West Germany's Seebohn Act which outlawed wooden-bodied cars—have changed all that. Some anachronisms do remain in passenger service, such as the horse-car trailers used in Innsbruck, and other old cars have been retired to the works fleet, but generally the old standard car is a thing of the past. And where a tramway has closed, little remains to show that it was ever there—no great earthworks, no station buildings, only perhaps the odd length of rail buried under the tarmac or the occasional overhead support. Inevitably in a public street the rest has to go, and few forms of transport can leave so little sign of their passing than the ever-humble tram.

BIBLIOGRAPHY

TRAMWAYS IN GENERAL

Clark D. K. *Tramways, Their Construction and Working* (1878, 1894)

Cole W. H. *Light Railways at Home and Abroad* (1899)

Davies W. J. K. *Light Railways* (1964)

Dover A. T. *Electric Traction* (1917, 1937)

Dunbar C. S. *Buses, Trolleys and Trams* (1967)

Joyce J. (ed) *Modern Tramway Review* (1964)

Klapper C. *The Golden Age of Tramways* (1961, Newton Abbot 1974)

Light Railway Transport League. *The Electric Railway Number of Cassier's Magazine* (1899, reprinted 1960)

Modern Tramway

Tramway Review

Whitcombe H. A. *History of the Steam Tram* (South Godstone 1954)

BRITISH TRAMWAYS

Blacker K. C. *The Felthams* (Blackpool 1962)

Bett W. H. & Gilham J. C. *Great British Tramway Networks* (Third Edition 1957)

Brearley H. *Tramways in West Yorkshire* (South Godstone 1960)

Brook R. *The Tramways of Huddersfield* (Huddersfield 1959)

Coonie I. M. & Clark R. R. *The Tramways of Paisley and District* (Glasgow 1954)

Cormack I. L. *Green Goddesses Go East: a brief history of the ex-Liverpool trams in Glasgow 1953–1960* (Glasgow 1961)

Cormack I. L. *Seventy-five Years on Wheels: The History of Public Transport in Barrow-in-Furness* (Glasgow 1960)

Gentry P. W. *Tramways of the West of England* (Second Edition 1960)

Hearse G. S. *Tramways of the City of Carlisle* (Corbridge 1962)

Hunter D. L. G. 'The Edinburgh Cable Tramways', *The Journal of Transport History*, 1 (Leicester 1953–4)

Jackson-Stevens E. *British Electric Tramways* (Newton Abbot 1971)

Joyce J. *Tramway Twilight: the Story of British Tramways from 1945 to 1962* (1962)

Kidner R. W. *The London Tramcar 1861–1952* (Lingfield 1965)

Lee C. E. *The Swansea and Mumbles Railway* (South Godstone 1954)

Markham R. *Public Transport in Ipswich* (Ipswich 1970)

Mc Neill D. B. *Ulster Tramways and Light Railways* (Belfast 1966)

Palmer G. S. & Turner B. R. *Blackpool by Tram* (Blackpool 1968)

Pearson F. K. *Isle of Man Tramways* (Newton Abbot 1970)

Wilson G. *London United Tramways, A History 1894–1933* (1971)

TRAMWAYS IN EUROPE, AMERICA and ELSEWHERE

Addison G. W. 'Memorandum on Light Railways in Belgium', *The Electrical Engineer*, 4 January 1895

Campenhoudt P. Van. *Le Musee Vicinal de Schepdaal* (Brussels 1963)

Centro Culturale dell'Azienda Tranviaria Municipale di Milano. *Cento Anni di Trasporti Publici a Milano* (Milan 1961)

Eisenbahnfreunde Hannover. *Die Geschichte der Strassenbahn in Hannover* (Hannover 1967)

Gragt F. Van Der *Europe's Greatest Tramway Network* (Leiden 1968)

Kahn E. *Cable Car Days in San Francisco* (California 1944)

Kingsborough L. S. *The Horse Tramways of Adelaide and its Suburbs 1875–1907* (Adelaide 1967)

Mensdorf J. & Reichenbach K. *75 Jahre Strassenbahn Plauen* (Dresden 1969)

Rowsome F. & Maguire S. D. *Trolley Car Treasury* (New York 1956)

Taplin M. R. *Tramways of Western Germany* (1971)

Wiedenbauer A. & Hoyer H-J. *Fahrt in die Zukunft, Die Geschichte der Frankfurter Strassenbahn* (Frankfurt-am-Main 1968)

Willemsen B. *The ABC of Tramways* (Doetinchem 1959)

ACKNOWLEDGEMENTS

I am happy to acknowledge the assistance, freely and generously given, which I have received from various official bodies, particularly the administrations of the following tramway or transport undertakings: Basle, Edinburgh, Frankfurt-am-Main, Ghent, Glasgow, Gothenburg, Hanover, Massachusetts Bay, Milan, Melbourne, Munich, New Orleans, Oslo, Pittsburgh Allegheny County, San Francisco, Shaker Heights, SNCV Belgium, Toronto, and Zurich, also the Budapest Museum of Communication, Hull Museum of Transport, Japan Information Centre, Stirling Public Library, Ulster Folk Museum and Ulster Museum.

My debt to *Modern Tramway* and its contributors is very great indeed, particularly in respect of the later chapters, for which I am grateful to the editor and to Ian Allan Ltd.

Personal debts of gratitude are owed to Mr J. S. Nicholson, for information and photographs relating to the City of Hull tramways, to Mrs F. M. Buckley, for assistance with translations, and especially to Mr Peter Cooke for producing most of the line drawings. Both he and my wife were instrumental in persuading me to begin work, but it is to my wife that I owe the greatest debt, for her patient encouragement and help at every stage of writing. Photographs and drawings not acknowledged individually are by the author, or in the case of page 80 from his collection.

R. J. BUCKLEY

INDEX

The index is divided into two parts. Part I lists tramway systems by country and by place, except for some interurbans, which are listed either individually or under a general heading. Part II covers general subjects. Page numbers in italic refer to illustrations.

PART I

PART II